WORTH CELEBRATING

You can probably count on the fingers of one hand the number of Christian books that have outlived the life of their author. Celebration of Discipline will be one of them, and Worth Celebrating will tell you why.

Mimi Dixon helps us fall in love with Jesus again, as if for the first time, and she rekindles an affection for the book that sparked a movement for spiritual formation right across the world.

JAMES CATFORD,
founding chair of The Center for Christianity
and Public Life, literary advisor to the Dallas Willard Estate,
and ministry team member of Renovaré

Who knew a book about a book could be a page-turner or that the story of a movement could be so moving? Mimi Dixon's ability to blend the keen insight of an analytical historian with the contagious passion of a transformed participant makes Worth Celebrating a captivating read. I reached the Epilogue not only awash in gratitude for what God has done in the "ripple effects" of Celebration of Discipline but also brimming with fresh hope at what God might yet do.

CAROLYN ARENDS,
recording artist, author,
and Renovaré Director of Education

Mimi Dixon has written a wonderful book biography of Richard Foster's Celebration of Discipline. It is more than a book biography, though. Richard appears frequently sharing his thoughts; new photographs are presented; we learn about the vision and beginning of Renovaré, and valuable appendices add much to Mimi's presentation, some written by Richard. This is a thoroughly researched, insightful, delightful book. Those who have already read Celebration of Discipline will enjoy it, and those who haven't are handed a key to open the treasure chest that Celebration of Discipline contains.

CHRIS HALL,
former Renovaré President,
author of *A Different Way* and *The Mystery of God*

Miriam Dixon writes of readers who purchased a copy of Celebration of Discipline and shelved it unopened. I, too, fall into that category. I purchased my copy at a discount bookstore after having a strong urge that it should be in my library. Two years later, recovering from burnout as a busy pastor, wife, and mother, Celebration lured me, this time as a healing companion. I enjoyed reading Dr. Dixon's history of Celebration and the inclusion of our dear friend Richard's reflections on his younger self. My one word of advice is to pull out your copy of Celebration of Discipline so that once you've read Worth Celebrating, it will be easily at hand. They are lovely companions on the way!

JUANITA RASMUS,
founder of The Art Project-Houston,
cofounder of Bread of Life, and author of *Learning to Be: Finding Your Center After the Bottom Falls Out*

Writing in a winsome, inviting, and down-to-earth style, Mimi Dixon helps us to see why Richard Foster's classic Celebration of Discipline is well worth celebrating. As she chronicles the remarkable story behind the book's origins, describes its transformative effects on individuals around the world, and recounts how it sparked into being the ever-growing spiritual formation movement throughout the evangelical world, Mimi also whets our appetite to cooperate with God in the ongoing transformation of our lives into the image of Christ. Celebration of Discipline, as Mimi observes, lit a fire in our world. I have a hunch that this book will fan this fire into even greater flame as it warms the hearts of readers into a deeper and more whole-hearted love for God and those around us.

TREVOR HUDSON,
Methodist Church of Southern Africa
and author of *Seeking God: Finding Another Kind of Life with Saint Ignatius and Dallas Willard*

WORTH CELEBRATING

A Biography of Richard J. Foster's
Celebration of Discipline

MIRIAM M. DIXON

IB

BARCLAY PRESS
Newberg, OR 97132

Worth Celebrating

A Biography of Richard J. Foster's *Celebration of Discipline*

©2024 by Miriam M. Dixon

Barclay Press, Inc.
Newberg, Oregon
www.barclaypress.com

All rights reserved. No part may be reproduced
for any commercial purpose by any method without
permission in writing from the copyright holder.

Printed in the United States of America

Cover and page design by Mareesa Fawver Moss

Cover photo by Kimon Maritz

Author photo: Bettinger Photography in Denver, Colorado

ISBN 978-1-59498-140-1

This book biography is dedicated to all those whose lives have been transformed by the *Celebration of Discipline.*

Contents

PART III: ONGOING TRANSFORMATIVE INFLUENCE

Letter to My Younger Self

—Richard J. Foster

Dear Richard,

This letter comes from your older self (some forty plus years into the future) regarding how you did in your writing of *Celebration of Discipline,* plus a few counsels about the years that are ahead. Let me begin with the writing itself.

First of all, I am astonished at how much you got right. This, I think, is a good indication that God was with you in the writing because there is simply no way you could have thought up all those things on your own. It reminds me of the time D. L. Moody was on a three-month preaching tour across England, and a skeptic followed him to see if he could expose "this commoner." Finally, he confronted Moody saying, "Mr. Moody I have been tracking you for the past three months, attending every one of your meetings, and I have concluded that God *must* be with you because there is absolutely nothing in your own abilities that could account for the results you are having." Moody, I rather imagine, was pleased by this report.

You, I know, were keenly aware when you wrote *Celebration* in 1978 that you were right on the hinge of a major cultural shift. I am pleased with how well you navigated your way through such a sea change, speaking truth to power in a genuinely chaotic time. Good for you! I am even more impressed at how those words written back then speak so forcefully into today's cultural context. Isn't it good of God to anticipate its relevancy across the decades! May this be true for many more decades to come.

I'm so glad you redeemed the word "discipline" for contemporary life, making it clear that discipline is what produces genuine liberation and is thus a cause for celebration. You have often taught that "the disciplined person is the person who can do what needs to be done *when* it needs to be done. Such a person is response-able . . . able to respond appropriately in any given situation." Yes, indeed. It was an important word for such an erratic and undisciplined time. And it is equally needed today.

By applying this central concept to the spiritual life, you were then able to introduce the spiritual Disciplines to a culture that had lost these time-honored means of grace for our growth into Christlikeness. I'm so glad you did this. People today really do need to recover a theology of spiritual growth that has been proven to work in the midst of the harsh realities of daily life. By God's grace, you have helped lead the way in this recovery.

Now, I would like to give you a few counsels for the years ahead. When you were in the midst of writing *Celebration* you, I know, had an "opening" about the future—how this book would usher you into a whole diversity of denominations and peoples around the world. Wisely you never said a word about this to anybody; I remind you of it now only to prepare you for what is to come.

Your original "opening" was spot on. With the publication of *Celebration* you will receive a flood of invitations and speaking opportunities . . . far more than you will possibly be able to fulfill. Don't get too caught up in all the energy and excitement of this. Keep your focus on the people, those precious people who long to grow in grace. Look straight into their eyes and listen prayerfully to their stories until you can feel their sorrow and pain. Only then will you be able to share the wonderful news of Jesus as their ever-present Teacher and Friend.

I suggest you accept only a few select invitations. Only in this way can you be truly present to the deeper needs of people. If you run yourself ragged going here and there, you will be of no benefit to anyone. Besides, the way of Christ is opposed to the religion of "the big deal."

Do treasure your times with Carolynn. She is going to sacrifice immensely in order for the message of *Celebration* to reach far and wide. So, take long walks together. View the countryside and smell the flowers. Oh, and do talk with her. Frankly, you tend to clam up when you need to open up and share your heart. Value a long marriage together.

The same counsel goes for the kids, Joel and Nathan. Take genuine interest in the things they care about. Only then will you earn the right to share your thoughts and counsel with them. Now, if Joel ever shares his concern about serving in the military, rest easy with your pacifist leanings and focus instead on his love of structure and order and his creative leadership for the good of others. And, oh, if Nathan ever asks you to climb 14,000 foot, mountains with him, do say YES! You both will gain more than you can ever imagine from the experience.

You have developed a warm friendship with Bill Vaswig and Dallas Willard. Don't ever let go of these relationships, even if you live great distances from each other. They will stabilize you, and in time, they will become your deepest, most lasting friends. In addition, build a team around you of like-minded people who will help you in this spiritual formation work. The task is far too great for you to accomplish alone.

When you are traveling and speaking, you will come across dear folk who are overly impressed with you. Don't take it too seriously. They mean well—just gently turn them from yourself to Jesus, their present Teacher.

I am afraid that all of this is going to put you in the spotlight for awhile. I know that this is something you have never desired nor sought after. However, I encourage you not to view this in a negative light. Rather, find ways to use your platform for the good of others, even giving them a platform when it is right and good.

Now, I don't want you to be surprised when folks misunderstand what you are teaching and turn the Disciplines into soul-destroying legalisms. I don't know why this is, but it just seems that people continually gravitate toward twisting such life-giving graces into such deadly legalisms. Some quite serious types can even master the mechanics of the Disciplines without ever experiencing the deep inner formation of heart and mind and soul that the Disciplines intend to guide us into. The point, as you know, is not the Disciplines in themselves but the with-God life they direct us toward.

I know, I know, you warned people against legalism in *Celebration*. But you are going to have to beat this drum over and over again until you become tired of talking about it.

One dimension of this soul-destroying legalism I want you to watch out for is what might be described as "liturgical legalism." Of course, there is nothing wrong with the various liturgies we have for embodying the "treasure" so long as our constant focus is on Jesus, the "treasure."[1] But the moment our focus is on the liturgies rather than Jesus and the life formation he brings, we are in danger of liturgical legalism. Such exclusive focus on the "vessel" will eventually lead to a kind of magic religion, which undermines the true role of liturgy. Instead, our focus always needs to be on the inward character formation that results from learning to walk daily in the ways of Christ. We are constantly looking for the marks of "love, joy, peace, patience, kindness, goodness, faithfulness, gentleness, and self-control" to be taking over the deep, interior habit structures of our life (Gal. 5:22–23).

Rigidity is the great enemy to the abundant *zoé* life that Jesus offers. But, Richard, rather than rigidity, I do encourage you to

14

live daily with Jesus, "light as a feather, fluid as water, innocent as a child, responding to every movement of grace like a floating balloon," to use the words of Jean-Pierre de Caussade.

I'm sure you already know this on some level, but I want you to be prepared for the attacks that will come against the message of *Celebration*. And against you personally. You will be amazed at how people will distort and disfigure what you are trying to say. Just remember, words have meaning more or less—more when people trust you and less when they don't. My counsel is to not even try to answer these attacks. Rest easy. You can trust God to watch out for your reputation.

One final matter, and this will probably to be difficult for you to hear. Frankly, Richard, you are trying too hard to be heroic in the spiritual life. Friendship with Jesus does not come by gritting your teeth but by falling in love. So, I would urge you to relax a bit, learn to be playful, and, by all means, laugh a lot. And, on occasion, follow the wisdom of Psalm 150 and break out the lute and the harp, the tambourine and the pipe, the clanging cymbals and the loud clashing cymbals, and throw a party in the presence of the Lord.

Peace and joy,
Richard

INTRODUCTION

A Word to the Reader

You hold in your hands a book about a book. This well-written and insightful "book biography" by Reverend Doctor Miriam M. Dixon extends the well-documented impact of *Celebration of Discipline: The Path to Spiritual Growth,* by Richard J. Foster. *Celebration* was named one of the top ten best religious books of the twentieth century[2] and has been in print for forty-five years in hardcover with no US paperback edition in sight. It has been translated into thirty-three languages, has sold millions of copies around the world, and is credited with jump-starting the Protestant "spiritual formation" movement in the US, which even Wikipedia chronicles.[3]

Biographies of books are a fairly new phenomenon in scholarly and trade publishing. They emerged out of the scholarship of SHARP, the Society for the History of Authorship, Reading, and Publishing, founded in 1992 by Jonathan Rose, Simon Eliot, and Patrick Leary. This academic field is growing steadily as nearly a thousand scholars in literature, library science, and history around the world are studying the "history of the book." Many wonderful articles and books are emerging from their research efforts, but the "biography of the book" is the most visible result.

17

Princeton University Press has devoted an entire series to "Lives of Great Religious Books." These short volumes, most of them subtitled "A Biography," recount the complex and fascinating histories of important religious texts from around the world, such as *Mere Christianity* by C.S. Lewis, Bonhoeffer's *Letters and Papers from Prison*, and the Holy Koran. These stories of translation, adaptation, appropriation, and inspiration dramatically remind us that all great religious books are living things whose careers in the world can take the most unexpected turns.

Other notable contributions include Grove Atlantic's series "Books that Changed the World," featuring religion scholar Karen Armstrong's explication of Judaic and Christian sacred text in *The Bible: A Biography.* In contrast to Armstrong's textual and historical approach, independent SHARP scholar Priscilla Coit Murphy takes a social science perspective in her biography of the groundbreaking Rachel Carson book that launched the environmental movement in 1962. Murphy's *What A Book Can Do: The Publication and Reception of Silent Spring* is a leading title in the University of Massachusetts Press series "Studies in Print Culture and the History of the Book."

The book biography phenomenon has now spread well beyond scholarly contexts. Popping up from various presses are chronicles such as *The Ministry of Truth: The Biography of George Orwell's 1984* by Dorian Lynskey (Picador Books/ Pan MacMillan, 2019) and *So We Read On: How The Great Gatsby Came to Be and Why it Endures* by Maureen Corrigan (Little Brown, 2014). Both books give more attention to information

about the book's author than to the cultural impact of the book itself, which is what merits a biography.

I commend Miriam Dixon for her illuminating portrayal of how one book changed the landscape of late twentieth-century American religion.

Roy M. Carlisle

What a Book Can Do

> When you sell a man a book, you do not sell him just
> twelve ounces of paper, ink, and glue;
> you sell him a whole new life.
> —Christopher Morley

An unknown author writes an unlikely book and inadvertently sparks an improbable global movement.

The manuscript was written longhand on a yellow pad in a small Oregon town by a Quaker pastor describing twelve ancient Christian disciplines (the very definition of the term "unlikely").[4] But publishers at Harper & Row saw something special in what Richard Foster had written and took a risk.

The movement kindled by the book developed slowly, almost imperceptibly. But once it caught hold, it exploded into flame.

I Was There

I remember the moment like it was yesterday.

I wandered into a bookstore where my eye was drawn to a stack of red-jacketed books on a table, bearing the title,

Celebration of Discipline. My curiosity piqued by the incongruous pairing of "celebration" and "discipline," I picked up a copy and opened to the first chapter to read, "Superficiality is the curse of our age."

I caught my breath. "Superficiality" gave my restlessness a name. Having just completed a postgraduate degree in theology, my mind was chock-full of knowledge, yet there remained a persistent sense that something important was missing.

"The desperate need today," continued Richard, "is not for a greater number of intelligent people, or gifted people, but for deep people. The classical Disciplines of the spiritual life call us to move beyond surface living into the depths. They invite us to explore the inner caverns of the spiritual realm."[5]

Feeling a flicker of hope that perhaps I had found the help I needed, I purchased the book and read it straight through. As I put what I was learning into practice, *Celebration of Discipline* sparked in me a fire. It grounded me spiritually, introduced me to a company of like-minded companions eager to grow in Christlikeness, and shaped the community of faith that I led for three and a half decades. The book delivered solidly on its bold invitation to transformation.

CHANGING TIMES

Celebration of Discipline was conceived during a period in history that Charles Dickens might describe as being the best of times and the worst of times. From its inception, American culture had been linked to Christian faith and values. We were "one nation under God, indivisible, with liberty and justice for all." The 1950s and early '60s saw the peak years of American churchgoing, when 70 percent of citizens attended church. But as the decade of the '60s stretched on, values and perspectives that had long been accepted as foundational to American faith and life began to come into question.

As the decade of the '70s emerged, Americans were hopeful that things would return to normal. But it was not to be. Life carried on as people rushed to and from school and work and church on Sundays, but like a faint scent carried on a breeze or the few flakes of snow that fall before a blizzard, the feeling grew that something was amiss.

As tension mounted and division proliferated, a Quaker pastor in a small town in Oregon published a book. Characteristic of a well-timed intervention, the book named what was at stake and offered a time-tested corrective.

THE POWER OF A BOOK

Books uniquely possess the ability to expose invisible obstacles, eliciting from readers a broad range of responses. Some readers welcome the revelation, seizing the corrective offered with gratitude, while others find fault both in the analysis and proffered solution.

Consider Rachel Carson's shattering exposé *Silent Spring*, which prompted an investigation into the unregulated use of pesticides and resulted in the creation of the Environmental Protection Agency. In her biography of *Silent Spring*, Priscilla Coit Murphy claims, "On occasion, the impact of individual books has been woven into social, cultural, or political history."[6]

When *Celebration of Discipline* spotlighted the superficiality that had come to characterize Christianity, it ignited the spiritual formation movement by prescribing the ancient spiritual practices as the necessary corrective. Michael Maudlin, religion publisher at HarperCollins, acknowledges, "People do not remember how Christians thought about spiritual formation in Christ before *Celebration of Discipline* was published. Most everybody now thinks it is natural for evangelicals to practice spiritual Disciplines. But it was not always so. *Celebration of Discipline* serves as a wonderful window into how a book can change a subculture."[7]

As it turns out, the book that became so influential was itself influenced by books.

CHEW AND DIGEST

Lord Chancellor Sir Francis Bacon famously said that while some books are to be tasted and others to be swallowed, there are a few which must be carefully chewed and digested.

Richard Foster had been deeply influenced as a teenager by Dietrich Bonhoeffer's seminal book, *The Cost of Discipleship*. So, when Professor Arthur Roberts introduced him to the writings of the devotional masters, Richard chewed and digested every one of those old books he could find. "We need to learn from these members of our historic family," asserts Eugene Peterson, "who lived lives similar to what we are living and lived them well."[8] In so doing, warned C. S. Lewis, we must be mindful of our approach. "We can look *at* a subject from another—and usually alien—point of view, which gives us ultimate authority over the subject; or we can look *along* it, allowing the subject itself to illumine the world for us."[9]

Following the beam of spiritual light streaming from the martyrs, mystics, ascetics, and reformers, Richard began to view the tumultuous time in which he was living in a fresh, new light. The ancient writers understood that the goal of life in this world is not ease, prosperity, and success but rather a deepening intimacy with God assisted by means of the spiritual Disciplines. His imagination set on fire, Richard shared what he was learning with bestselling author Elton Trueblood, who encouraged him to put his developing perspective into print.

"For as good as the spoken word may be, the printed word is better, because the printed word can be studied. Its glory lies in its freedom from mere transitoriness."[10] British publisher Edward England agreed, "When the missionary has gone on furlough, the sermon ended, the church doors locked, the radio program concluded, the television picture faded, the book remains."[11] "No other agency can penetrate so deeply, abide so persistently, witness so daringly, and influence so irresistibly," confirms Charles Watson, "as the printed page."[12] This is the power of a book.

"It is a simple fact," Richard reasoned, "that a large number of people can be reached for a sustained period of time through books. Compared to other means of communication, a book has greater permanence and precision. A book is a 'minister' that can be available to people any time of the day or night."[13]

Picking up his pen, Richard sketched the outline of what would become *Celebration of Discipline*.

THE INDISPENSABLE GUIDE

When a reporter asked G. K. Chesterton what one book he would want to have along if stranded on a desert island, he answered, "a practical guide to shipbuilding, of course." *Celebration of Discipline* is read again and again because Elton Trueblood was right—the Disciplines have proven to be as helpful to modern Christians as a practical guide to shipbuilding would be to a person marooned on a desert island.

"If there was just one book that I could have as an extra with my Bible," confided a journalist from *Christian Woman Magazine*, "it would be *Celebration of Discipline* by Richard Foster. This is a book that I doubt I shall ever put away as having either attained to what it puts forward or not finding something new to challenge me in my continuing spiritual life."[14] "The book I'm spending time with again this Lent first appeared in 1978, and it seems to be heading toward contemporary classic status," stated a reporter from *Voice of the Southwest. "Celebration of Discipline* by Richard J. Foster ranks among the best books on Christian spirituality in the modern world."[15] Evangelist Tommy Tyson agreed with this assessment, *"Celebration of Discipline* should be in the library of every Christian and should be read and studied on a regular basis."[16]

In October of 2006, *Christianity Today* polled dozens of evangelical leaders to learn which books they felt had, over the last half century, altered the way that American evangelicals pray, gather, talk, and reach out. Of the fifty most-influential books, readers ranked *Celebration of Discipline* as number eleven.

Celebration of Discipline was exceeding all expectations. Its published message found its way into diverse denominational contexts and countries around the world, reaching audiences well beyond the limited scope of speaking engagements, interviews, and published articles. It had become an indispensable guide. Which explains the inscription Chris McFadden found scribbled on the inside cover of a well-marked copy of *Celebration of Discipline* that he found in his pastor's study: "Read this FIRST!"[17]

Doctrine Is Not Enough

When *Celebration of Discipline* began flying off the shelves, bookstore managers asked, "What accounts for the sudden uptick of interest in spiritual subjects?" Phyllis Tickle, religion editor for *Publisher's Weekly*, had a ready answer. She identified 1965 as the year when specific interest in books about spirituality began to emerge.[18] But late in the decade of the seventies, Tickle noticed a new development.

Following the publication of *Celebration of Discipline* in 1978, dozens of new books exploring the early church fathers and devotional masters began to spike sales. By 1992, spirituality as a category of publishing was approaching triple-digit annual growth with over twenty-five hundred books about meditation, prayer, and techniques for spiritual growth in print. "From M. Scott Peck's quintessential bestseller, *The Road Less Traveled*, to the almost equally immortal books of Richard Foster on spiritual formation," Tickle reported, "all are selling well."[19] She theorized that sales were being driven by the fact that much of what contemporary Christianity offered was not leading people into the depths of God.

"All of us at some point discover," observes author Curt Thompson, "that our theology, even if it is neatly packaged, doesn't on its own keep us from losing our tempers with our children or becoming rigid and self-righteous during the conflicts we have with our spouses, our coworkers, or our children's teachers. We find that what we are told to believe does not match our intuitive experience and often lacks relevance in our daily lives. As things seem to get worse, not better, we sometimes begin to give up the possibility that we will ever become what we want to become."[20] Gerald L. Sittser soberly agreed. "We are feeling restless and dissatisfied. We say to ourselves, 'there must be more than this!'"[21]

Trending sales were compelling Tickle to conclude, "Christians seem to be saying it is not enough to know only in one's head. Doctrine is not enough, will never be enough. The sense of something deeply integral having been lost has become a shared, focused one in American culture."[22]

Eugene Peterson observed, "Like a child exploring the attic of an old house on a rainy day, discovering a trunk full of treasure and then calling all his brothers and sisters to share the find, Richard Foster 'found' the spiritual Disciplines that the modern world stored away and forgot, and has excitedly called us to celebrate them. For they are, as Foster shows us, the instruments of joy, the way into mature Christian spirituality and abundant life."[23]

Desperate to experience a deeper life with God, droves of Christians purchased copies of *Celebration of Discipline* and bought extras to give to their friends.

SPECIAL MENTION

In 2008, HarperOne compiled a list of their bestselling books on religion, spirituality, and personal growth with combined sales of more than ten million copies. Singling out *Celebration of Discipline* for special mention, Harper acknowledged, "Foster may not have realized the revolution he was launching. He has challenged us to see Christian faith, not just as a system of doctrinal information but as a life of spiritual transformation, a way of life formed by disciplined spiritual practices. The lasting influence, we believe, will be measured in decades and centuries, not months or years."[24]

In the preface to the fortieth anniversary edition of the best-selling book, Richard Foster wrote, "Forty years ago, there was an abysmal ignorance of how we grow in grace, entering into ever fuller and deeper Christlikeness. I penned *Celebration of Discipline* in response to this crying need. The [reception] was a genuine surprise. And overwhelming. The hunger for real, transforming power was greater than I ever could have imagined. Once people realized that progress in character formation is actually possible, they were seized with genuine hope and encouragement. Vast numbers of ordinary folk have taken into their own lives Disciplines of the spiritual life that reflect the overall life of Jesus himself. And they have indeed discovered these spiritual Disciplines to be the means of God's grace for the formation and transformation of heart and mind and spirit and body and soul. They have actually made progress forward in the spiritual life. I thank God!"[25]

Some books initiate interventions. Some books spark movements. *Celebration of Discipline* accomplishes both. It is a modern classic.

A Modern Classic

Some might argue that to rank as a "classic," a book must be in continuous print for at least one hundred years. In reality, age has very little to do with it. On occasion, a more recent publication comes along that carries an uncommon presence and power and clearly warrants this coveted distinction. At the turn of the century, *Christianity Today* ranked *Celebration of Discipline* among the top ten of the one hundred books that "had shaped contemporary religious thought." The accompanying notation read, "After Foster finishes each spiritual Discipline, you not only know what it is, why it's important, and how to do it—you *want* to do it."[26]

Largely by word of mouth, *Celebration of Discipline* had found its way into scores of personal libraries and pastors' studies.

Leaders from Christian universities, conference centers, and local churches representing a broad range of denominational affiliation read and recommended the book to their membership. Mainline Protestant and evangelical, Pentecostal and Charismatic, Roman Catholic and Orthodox readers credited the book for guiding them into real, substantive spiritual transformation and maturity in Christ.

It must, however, be acknowledged from the start that there are some inherent limitations in telling the story of a book such as *Celebration of Discipline*. Ordinarily the focus of attention rests upon its public reception supported by book reviews and sales figures. These are important data points, yet I would argue that this is not where *Celebration of Discipline*'s most powerful influence may be found. American historian George Marsden contends that over time classics like *Celebration of Discipline* literally take on a life of their own. Or it may be more accurate to say that they take on several million lives as the book intersects with the actual experience of its readers.[27]

There is no adequate way to quantify all these stories because readers' reactions range anywhere from casual indifference to crediting the book for initiating a profound inner transformation. *Celebration of Discipline* has been recommended, read, set aside, or embraced by so many people in so many situations in so many parts of the world that it would be impossible to obtain a comprehensive measure of its effect, not to mention the transformative influence of the many whose lives have been changed and are changing. The best we can do in the wake of such broad and varied influence is to share some representative stories—beginning with my own.

BUTTONS IN BUTTONHOLES

In 1978 *Celebration of Discipline* became my spiritual guide. I practiced the Disciplines, fully expecting that this would result in a deepening intimacy with God; I was not disappointed. I felt

Mother Theresa – 3 hrs. of Prayer
Calloused knees

closely connected to God and consciously aware of God's presence both in and around me.

But then—I got busy. The first of many casualties in my overcrowded ministry was my daily practice of the Disciplines. I told myself that I didn't have time to sit quietly before God—listening, noticing, responding. I told myself that I would get to it later. I told myself that I was busy doing God's work, which somehow justified my neglect.

I didn't notice the effects at first. They developed slowly over time, manifesting in an increased anxiety and restlessness. I worried about my work. I worried about my relationships. I struggled with a growing sense of isolation. As signs of burnout began to appear, I knew I had to do something.

Deciding that what I needed was a spiritual infusion, I signed up for a two-week intensive class with Dallas Willard. When the opportunity for an individual appointment was offered, I put my name on the list. When my turn came, I anxiously shared what was happening and asked Dr. Willard for his advice. With a reassuring smile, he replied, "You know what to do! Practice the Disciplines!"

Entwining his fingers, Dr. Willard explained, "You might picture the Disciplines as buttons in buttonholes. The Disciplines connect this world with the Kingdom of God. They keep God close as you go about your everyday life. Practice the Disciplines and see if this does not solve your problem."

C.S. Lewis called this the principle of first and second things. In a letter to Dom Bede Griffiths, he explained, "Jesus tells us to *'seek first the Kingdom of God and his righteousness, and all these things will be added to you.'* When we put first things first, we get second things thrown in. But if we put second things first, we lose both first and second things."[28] I experienced burnout when I allowed the "second things" of my ministry to assume first place.

Taking Dallas Willard's advice, I reread *Celebration of Discipline* and resumed my daily practice of the Disciplines. Like inserting buttons into buttonholes, the Disciplines kept me closely connected to God in the busy activity of ministry. And in the twenty-two years of pastoral ministry that followed, I never again experienced symptoms of burnout.

Practice of the Disciplines has had a similar effect on Jodie Muller. "I purchased a copy of *Celebration of Discipline* years ago and just recently picked it up to read. Practice of the Disciplines has helped me to reframe my experience of turmoil and loss in light of God's loving plan and provision; they are a means of grace."[29]

Anglican Bishop Todd Hunter also purchased—and promptly shelved—an early edition of *Celebration of Discipline*. Then one day, during an extended period of spiritual drought, Hunter went to his bookshelf to retrieve Richard's book. This was a leading of the Holy Spirit, Hunter says, "because reading *Celebration of Discipline* introduced me to the classic spiritual Disciplines and started me on a personal path to transformation. *Celebration of Discipline* was a springboard, a launching pad—the mustard seed that became the bush of my life—the spark that lit a fire causing an explosion. *Celebration* is not a book of information—it is practical. It rescued me."[30]

QUESTIONS WORTH PURSUING

To say that *Celebration of Discipline* has exerted a life-changing, perspective-altering influence is evident from countless stories like these and from the fact that the book has been in continuous publication since 1978. It has sold well above two million hardback copies in English (Harper has never released a paperback edition) and has been translated into thirty-three languages. Using current book sales as a measure, this modern spiritual classic is in as much demand today as it ever has been.

So, what accounts for *Celebration of Discipline*'s persistent popularity? What is the story behind the story? We will divide our investigation into three movements: the book's creation, reception, and ongoing transformative influence.

Part I: Creation

We will begin by establishing the historic context for the book. What was it in the cultural and religious fallout of the '60s and '70s that captured Richard Foster's attention, instilling in him a captivating vision of what is possible in a living relationship with God? What rich treasures did his quest reveal that compelled Richard to put his discoveries into print for the sake of others?

Part II: Reception

Publishers from both sides of the Atlantic Ocean will take us behind the scenes. How was the book launched and initially received? We will review testimonials that account for the book's enthusiastic reception and appraise the negative analysis of critics who publicly denounced the book's content. We will conclude with a scholarly summation.

Part III: Ongoing Transformative Influence

In the final section of the book, we will view different ways that the spiritual formation movement sparked by *Celebration of Discipline* has continued to develop and spread. We will examine evidence suggesting that the book's influence extends well beyond the movement it sparked. We will conclude by imagining what this influence may be and where it leads.

A STORY OF CHANGED LIVES

I was there at the beginning. The story of *Celebration of Discipline* is my story.

Mine is a life that is changed. Maybe yours is too. Or perhaps it can be.

— PART I —

Creation

Every book originates out of a complex mixture of culture, history, personal experience, and more. And, if it is a book of genuine substance, it will also provide a prophetic voice speaking into the "cultural stew" of the day. We now turn to this historic and societal context out of which *Celebration of Discipline* emerged.

CHAPTER 1

A Long Look Back

On December 29, 1962, Carl Bridenbaugh, president of the American Historical Society, delivered his annual address to a roomful of historians. Acknowledging the cataclysmic cultural shift that was so obviously happening, he gave it a name, "The Great Mutation." More than ever, he urged his colleagues, "it has become necessary for us to focus on the several historic stages on which men have played a part," because the "long-range point of view the best historians take gives them and their readers an advantage that no other study of human society can impart. We owe it to the entire past, the past which supports us, to understand it to the best of our abilities; and we owe it to the future to make this past understandable."

Bridenbaugh was one of the first predictive historians to speak so bluntly about what he was seeing and its place in the broader context of history.[31] Yet his cautionary warning went unheeded until, like a pot on a stove, almost overnight the contents went from hot to boiling, causing even the most casual observer to admit that something dramatic and inescapable was happening. What Bridenbaugh and his fellow historians glimpsed was now in full public view.

Unprepared, Americans were caught flat-footed as intellectually, politically, economically, culturally, sociologically, religiously, psychologically—every part of how we are and how we live—was swirling in a maelstrom of change.

STORM CYCLES

We tend to forget that we live lives firmly embedded within the long arms of history, that our times are merely the continuation of, or sequel to, the times that belonged to our predecessors. Normally such naïve forgetfulness does not matter greatly in the grand scheme of things. But in something as dramatic and consequential as the cultural shift that became apparent in the sixties and appears to be accelerating with time, forgetfulness is not a virtue.

Might there be a historic precedent to help us understand how to approach and engage this tsunami of change? Phyllis Tickle, citing the predictive acuity of Carl Bridenbaugh, contends that understanding may be found in the broad context of history.[32]

The first major historic transition took place when Christianity was born. The birth, public ministry, teachings, crucifixion, and resurrection of Jesus Christ caused even the epochs of human time to be redated into BC, Before Christ, and *anno Domini*, "in the year of our Lord"—and this by believers and nonbelievers alike. So cataclysmic was the transition, so complete, social historians have labeled it, "The Great Transformation."

Looking forward five hundred years from the Great Transformation to the sixth century, we find the "decline and fall of the Roman Empire." The storm surrounding this period thrust Europe into the Early Middle Ages. Through the prescience and spiritual acumen of leaders like Gregory the Great, Western culture and Christian faith was held in trust by Europe's convents and monasteries.

Five hundred years from the decline and fall of the Roman Empire places us in the eleventh century and what is known as the "Great Schism." The Western world spent a contentious and violent century and a half getting ready for the severance of East from West politically, militarily, economically, culturally, linguistically, intellectually, and of course, religiously. East and West would part company, and Europe would eventually see an ending of feudalism.

Move ahead five hundred years from the Great Schism, and we find ourselves squarely in the sixteenth century and what is called "The Great Reformation." Division and discontent within the Roman Catholic Church resulted in the birth of Protestant Christianity, with its gifts of rationalism and enlightenment upon which Western culture now stands.

An additional five hundred years brings us to our own place in history. If this way of understanding the past holds true, we are currently dead center in another of such events in Western history. Tickle reports that a growing number of contemporary theorists have reached this conclusion, calling this the "Fifth Turning."[33] The transition began in the twentieth century, as clouds gathered and the sky darkened, but this went largely unnoticed until, in the sixties, life as we know it was upended.

CHAPTER 2

Storms of Change

Those of us who did not live through the upheaval of the 1960s can hardly imagine the fear, anger, anxiety, and uncertainty that Americans endured as the landscape around them shifted. To assist our quest to understand what motivated Richard Foster to write *Celebration of Discipline*, a quick review of the sixties and seventies is in order.

THE 1960s—
THE DECADE WHEN EVERYTHING CHANGED[34]

At the beginning of the decade, when handsome, youthful John F. Kennedy was elected president, many Americans believed it was the dawn of a golden age. Optimism ran high. But by the end of the decade, it seemed like the nation was collapsing in on itself.

Without warning, the change descended on a population enjoying a period of unprecedented wealth, education, and opportunity. Television was in its infancy, bringing attention to public affairs in new ways. Images from across the nation and around the world were televised instantaneously into the living rooms of American families. Anyone who was alive in those years remembers vividly where they were and what they were doing on November 22, 1963, when the news flashed across the television screen that President Kennedy had been assassinated in Dallas, Texas. Suddenly everything was different. The future didn't look so promising.

With the volume of televised information increasing daily, almost exponentially, the population was soon overwhelmed by cascading events: the war in Vietnam and violent student protests, the Cold War with Russia and threat of nuclear holocaust, the burgeoning conflict in the struggle for racial justice and equality, the "peace-and-love" culture with its increasing drug use gaining momentum in Haight-Ashbury, the shocking political assassinations of Malcolm X, Martin Luther King Jr., and Robert F. Kennedy. When the Vietnam War finally ended in 1973, America's relief was overshadowed by the political scandal of Watergate, which dominated television and newspapers. In 1974, President Nixon resigned from the presidency.

Being so closely connected to these televised events generated a national sense of profound disorientation. Armed with the conviction that, as Americans, we each bear the responsibility to improve the future for our children, no one knew what to do. Uncertainty laid the foundation for what quickly became the most tumultuous and divisive decade to date in American history.

The summer of 1969 featured several large-scale events designed to rally people's spirits. Over six weekends, organizers of the Harlem Cultural Festival welcomed a combined audience of nearly 300,000 in Mount Morris Park to celebrate the vibrancy of Black music and culture. In August, a crowd of more than 400,000 young people descended on Yasgur's dairy farm in upstate New York to celebrate the peace-and-love movement in the Woodstock Music and Art Fair. In late July, NASA landed the first man on the moon. But even with the enthusiastic reception of these events, as the decade drew to a close, the nation's sense of community lay in tatters.

At mid-century, institutionalized Christianity had been front and center in American life. Young white couples moved to the suburbs and filled the pews on Sunday, establishing family and church as the twin pillars of respectability. Up until the sixties, the "Protestant establishment" (Episcopalians, Lutherans, Methodists, and Presbyterians) exerted uncontested social and political dominance. But now things began to shift.

The dawn of the sixties saw the development of a much more libertarian view of life. Women entered the workforce in numbers not seen since World War II. Divorce was readily available. Birthrates declined. People were more mobile than ever before, leading to family units that were much more varied and multicultural. "Everything was fab and groovy, and the church seemed part of a distant, old-fashioned past."[35]

Up until then, the average American child, whether Protestant or Roman Catholic, had been taught Bible stories at church and possessed a formative grasp of the religious and moral points contained in them. But as religious patterns shifted, America's younger generations became untethered from the parables and prophecies, interpretations and principles that supported the country's religious base.

The consequences of this were twofold. Some young people pursued spiritual engagement through traditional Christian sources. Others, hungry for a personalized spiritual experience not readily available through the established church, responded eagerly when the door to alternate forms of spirituality swung open. When Bill Moyers promoted a special televised PBS series featuring the teachings of Joseph Campbell, a popularized revival of mythology began to trend.[36]

For decades, institutional Christianity had preached a gospel emphasizing correct doctrine and moral conduct. With the notable exception of Pentecostal and Charismatic groups, there had been little teaching about a direct, experiential encounter with the Divine. With a range of religious alternatives now available for public consumption, including the recreational use of consciousness-expanding psychedelic drugs, the compounding spiritual effect was much nearer to a blizzard than a gentle snowfall. The religious world wobbled free of its axis.

A Gallup poll conducted in the winter of 1982 found that "interest in religion among Americans clearly appears to be on the rise."[37] However, pollster George Gallop warned, these results may not be as promising for established churches as it first seems.[38] Large numbers of Americans, churched and unchurched alike, agreed "most churches are not effective in helping people find meaning in life," while six in ten unchurched Americans affirmed that "churches and synagogues have lost the real, spiritual part of religion."

Institutional churches struggled to navigate the rapidly changing landscape, experimenting with coffee houses and contemporary forms of worship designed to attract young people. Four prominent evangelical leaders—Lloyd Ogilvie, Bruce Larson, Keith Miller, and Lyman Coleman—joined together to launch Faith at Work, a church-based small group movement. Their hope was that as parishioners studied the scriptures and shared openly in a confidential setting, prayed for one another, and held one another accountable, they would experience personal spiritual renewal, which, in turn, would renew the church at large. The small group movement had some success during the 1970s, but for the most part, the institutional church was reeling.

While the longing for an experiential relationship with God compelled some to explore alternative forms of spirituality, it drove others to search the scriptures for guidance.

A Fresh Outpouring

Father Dennis J. Bennett, rector of St. Mark's Episcopal Church in Van Nuys, California, had been meeting with a group of parishioners for some time, studying the New Testament book of Acts. During Holy Week in 1960, Bennett had a personal

surrounding world. Nature was his first introduction and lasting invitation to a creative God who delights in beauty.

THAT SILENT NIGHT

When Richard was ten years of age, the family moved to Garden Grove, California. His mother was kept busy raising three energetic sons, rabbits, and a flock of chickens, managing a large vegetable garden,

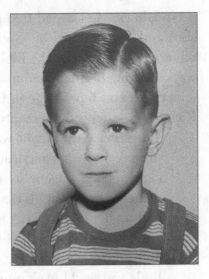

and teaching piano lessons to generate a little extra income. It was here that Richard, through the teaching and leadership of the nearby Alamitos Friends Church, was awakened to the life of the Christian community and to scripture.

Eugene and Jean Coffin were pastors of the Alamitos Friends Church; Eugene preached, and Jean played the organ and taught Sunday school. Under their faithful leadership and

without his conscious awareness, Richard learned many things about a life lived with God. He learned that God is active in our world today, communicating in fresh ways through our living and present Teacher, Jesus Christ. He learned that every person has value and worth to God. He learned that God chooses to mediate the Holy Spirit's transforming power through ordinary persons of widely varying temperaments and personalities. He learned that through the Holy Spirit, we are constantly surrounded by God's Light—illuminating, guiding, filling us. The stories in the Bible came alive to him in wonderful ways, exciting his imagination over the possibility of a close, interactive friendship with Jesus Christ. Then one Christmas Eve, Richard experienced the reality of this for himself.

> The service that night was simple enough with Jean playing the organ and leading us in familiar Christmas carols. Then Eugene sat in a large rocking chair and gathered us kids at his feet. He scooped up a little child and sat her on his lap. A holy hush seemed to cover us all, children and adults alike. Eugene looked at us, each one individually, lovingly, quietly. Then he took out his Bible and read Luke's rendition of the Christmas story. There were no dimming lights, no flickering candles, none of the things that are supposed to create just the right mood. It wasn't the outward, physical things at all. It was the holy hush that fell upon us. It was "the Presence in the midst." It was the breaking-in of the Shekinah of God. Even today, many years later, I vividly remember that silent night, that holy night.[46]

Richard's experience of God's holy presence prepared him for a profound and shattering glimpse into his own soul—his first conscious recognition of sin. It happened one afternoon as Richard followed his normal path home from school through a neighboring rancher's orange grove. He had walked that way many times before and never been tempted to take any fruit, but on this particular day he experienced a sudden urge to steal. Richard knew it was wrong, and as soon as he had picked the orange from the tree, he instantly threw it away, but in that moment, in that singular action, he glimpsed in himself a will that was in open rebellion against God.

Shattered by his capacity to do something that he knew was wrong, Richard ran home where he knelt by his bed. As he poured out his regret in confession, begging Jesus to forgive him and to help him to live a holy life, Richard confides, "I could sense myself passing through the flaming sword of God and entering into the overcoming life of Jesus, the Christ."

Rising to his feet, Richard spoke aloud to the empty room, "So this is what it means to be a Christian." No emotion accompanied this vivid awareness, just a strong assurance that he had passed from death into life. The very next morning Richard rose an hour early to read his Bible. Nobody had ever suggested that he do this; it just seemed a good thing to do. This practice became his daily routine.

Two Formative Experiences

During his teenage years, two formative experiences influenced Richard Foster's developing faith and relationship to Jesus Christ. The first was his active involvement in the Alamitos church youth group. "I gained my first understanding of the crucial importance of Christian community from that group."

Bill Freeman (the youth pastor) led the twenty or so young people in a dive-into-the-commentaries form of serious Bible study. They met weekly for two years to unpack Paul's theology in the book of Romans. As the students studied and debated the scriptures, Richard began to develop skill as a Bible teacher. Pastor Eugene helped him develop his first talk for the youth group based on Jesus' parable of the wheat and tares.

A second formative experience came at Quaker Meadow, a rustic camp in California's high Sierra Nevada Mountains. Pastor Eugene, who was a frequent speaker at the camp, invited the campers into an experiment in listening to God. This involved observing one hour of silence each day. Something of lasting value developed in Richard as he sat alone. Stillness came. At Quaker Meadow, Richard made, as he puts it, "my first stumbling efforts at prayer."[47] This was far and away the most essential lesson he learned for his own spiritual formation. Almost imperceptibly, Richard began slipping into the wisdom of the psalmist, "Be still and know that I am God."[48]

As a teenager, Richard describes himself as having been a zealous, perhaps *too* zealous, disciple of Jesus. A certain critical, judgmental spirit had crept in. Concerned that many contemporary Christians had succumbed to the prevailing culture, he bluntly declared, "We are to be an *alternative* to the culture, not captive to it!" Reflecting on that time, Richard recognizes that his concerns certainly had some truth to them, but they were also laced with legalism and rigidity. He had begun to seriously wonder if an authentic Christian life was even possible in our contemporary day and age.

FANNING THE FLAMES

The speaker at Quaker Meadow that summer, Ron Woodward, told the story of Dietrich Bonhoeffer and urged the campers to read *The Cost of Discipleship* (Richard still has his original tattered copy). Bonhoeffer described Jesus' Sermon on the Mount as a clarion call to a radical new understanding of discipleship that resulted in real, substantive change, a transformation of heart and mind and soul.

This idea captured Richard's imagination and fanned the flames of his developing passion for God. For in the religious culture of the time, "discipleship" described a program of reading the Bible, memorizing verses, and evangelistic training. It did not give sustained attention to character formation. What Bonhoeffer described was not a "program" at all. It was radical obedience to Jesus as the Master Teacher of life.

Richard Foster's reading of Bonhoeffer gave shape and substance to what he had been taught to believe in the Alamitos Friends Church: that Jesus is knowable and alive and present among his people—that it is possible to follow Jesus today as clearly and truly as did the original twelve disciples—learning from Jesus, following his example, living his life. Richard understood that we are not just *saved* by grace, we *live* by grace, and we *grow* by grace. Further, grace comes to us most often in the form of a cooperative relationship whereby God and we work together in partnership.

Bonhoeffer presented the classic Disciplines of the spiritual life as the central means by which the human personality is reformed—silence and solitude, simplicity and prayer, fasting and hiddenness—all of them practiced by Jesus. Followers of Jesus, Bonhoeffer asserted, are expected to practice these Disciplines as did he.

These ideas for Richard Foster were, as yet, in embryonic form, but they would grow and develop into a deep understanding of how the human heart and mind and soul are formed into the character of Jesus.

To sharpen his communication skills, Richard enrolled in a public speaking class and joined the debate team at Rancho Alamitos High School. He was elected president of the Bible club and frequently addressed the seven hundred or so students who filled one side of the school gymnasium before school on Thursday mornings. Quoting the famous dictum of René Descartes, "Cogito ergo sum" ("I think, therefore I am"), Richard would argue, "Because I *am*, because I *exist*, I must *decide*!" Once we consider all the options, he urged, deciding to follow Jesus as the Maestro of life is the most logical, compelling decision we can make.

The summer following his graduation from high school, Richard had another transformative experience. He and a handful of other young men accompanied pastor Homer Vail on a mission trip to the Inupiaq people in Kotzebue, Alaska, thirty miles above the Arctic Circle. Richard joined the group with a question in the back of his mind, "Is a life of Christian discipleship actually possible today?"

The Christian Inupiaq people he met that summer answered this question. In a culture far removed from his own, Richard witnessed what he was looking for. "It seemed to me that so many of the Inupiaq had died to self. They had died to position and status; they had died to pride and vainglory."[49] He now understood the spiritual Disciplines to be the means—transformation of character the unmistakable result.

GEORGE FOX COLLEGE AND BEYOND

Returning from Alaska, it was time for Richard to enroll in college. With his mother ill and frequently hospitalized, he secured a job to assist financially in his mother's support and enrolled in a local community college. One Sunday morning a couple from the Alamitos Friends Church, Bill and Alverna Cobb, invited Richard home for lunch following worship. They asked about his plans for college. When he described his situation, they asked, "If you could attend college anywhere, where would you go?" Without hesitation, Richard answered, "George Fox College!"

The Cobbs conferred with several other families in the church, and together they agreed to cover Richard's tuition at George Fox College. With the grateful support of his parents, Richard left the next Friday morning for Newberg, Oregon.

During those important developmental years at George Fox, philosophy Professor Arthur Roberts had a strong formative influence on Richard. "Arthur taught me so much more than philosophy; he taught me to value words and to treasure prayer."[50]

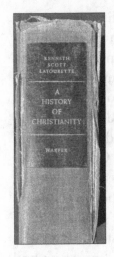

Perhaps the most influential moment came when Dr. Roberts encouraged Richard and a friend to enroll in a class he was teaching at a nearby college. The textbook was Yale historian Kenneth Scott LaTourette's monumental work, *A History of Christianity*. Dr. Robert's penetrating lectures into Christian history ignited in Richard a "furious love affair with the devotional masters" and established the foundation for what much later became *Celebration of Discipline*.

When Richard graduated from college, his supporters at the Alamitos Friends Church asked to know his plans. When Richard shared his desire to enroll as a full-time student at Fuller Theological Seminary in Pasadena, California, the group committed to extend their financial support. Richard supplemented his income by working part-time as a youth pastor at Alamitos Friends Church.

Richard's schedule left him little time to date, much less consider marriage, but that was about to change.

A DIVINE EPIPHANY

Through an unusual set of circumstances, Richard became reacquainted with one of his childhood friends, Jerry Williams, who was studying at Long Beach State College in Southern California. In the course of catching up, Jerry asked if Richard would "like a date with a neat Christian girl." Richard agreed, prompting Jerry to arrange for him to meet Carolynn Kerr (Jerry knew Carolynn from her active involvement with Intervarsity Christian Fellowship on the Long Beach State Campus). The plan was for Jerry and his fiancée to join Richard and Carolynn for a barbeque at the home where Richard was house-sitting and go afterward to Knott's Berry Farm.

Richard telephoned Carolynn to obtain directions to her home and promptly lost his notes, requiring a follow-up telephone conversation. When he called a third time to say he was delayed at work and would be late picking her up, all Carolynn said was, "You sound like an *interesting* person to meet."

Carolynn reports that she was amused by Richard's absent-mindedness but unconcerned. Having dated several non-Christian young men on campus, she had asked God to lead her to a committed Christian man who shared a passion for Jesus. A seminary student certainly showed promise, although Carolynn was not particularly interested in being a pastor's wife.

When Richard was finally on his way, he stopped at a gas station several miles from Carolynn's home to "spruce up and collect his thoughts." As he combed his hair, he suddenly had a strong sense of divine Presence and "heard" the unexpected words, "You are going to marry this woman."

Startled, Richard told himself, "Calm down! You've not even met this person yet!" Well, he was in for a very pleasant surprise. Carolynn was beautiful, smart, funny, and delightful. Something new was beginning to stir in Richard's heart.

As the evening unfolded, the impression Richard had received at the gas station grew pronounced and kept echoing in his mind. Even before taking Carolynn home, Richard had resolved to spend as much time with her as he possibly could. So, following that first date in early May, every weekend Richard drove fifty miles each way to see her. And, slowly, Carolynn adjusted to the notion of a life together in service to a congregation.

By September, Richard was ready to make his move. Wanting his proposal of marriage to be extra special, he arranged to take Carolynn and her mother (as chaperone) to Quaker Meadow for the weekend. The camping season had just ended, and the workers were readying the camp for the deep winter snows. While her mother stayed behind in the cabin, Richard took Carolynn to Inspiration Point, his special place high above the camp that featured a stunning view of the High

Sierra Mountains. He proposed; she accepted. Carolynn's parents approved, and in March of the following year, Richard and Carolynn were married.

For Richard, everything was coming up roses. He and Carolynn were happy; he would soon graduate from seminary, and he was optimistic about his future in pastoral ministry. Richard looked forward to the opportunity to "do great things for the kingdom of God."

Nothing could have prepared him for what he would experience in his first pastorate.

INTO THE DESERT

Having completed six years of postgraduate study, Richard graduated from Fuller Seminary in the spring of 1970 with a *Doctoris Theologiae Pastoralis*.[51] He accepted the invitation of the Woodlake Avenue Friends Church in the San Fernando Valley of Southern California to be their pastor. Confident that his efforts would result in substantial growth, Richard was unconcerned when the pastor he was replacing, Jim Hewitt, placed a sympathetic arm around his shoulder and stated, "Well, Richard, now it's your turn to be in the desert!"

Jim Hewitt's comment was prescient in several ways. First of all, things happen in the desert. The wilderness—spiritually speaking at least—is a place of encounter, a learning space, a laboratory of the soul. Second, in the providence of God, three influences would converge to change the direction of Richard's ministry—indeed, of his whole life.

The first influence was a sudden influx of genuinely needy people. Individuals struggling to navigate their lives and hungering for a deeper life with God flowed into the church like streams after a thunderstorm. Richard did his best to address their issues pastorally, but it soon became apparent that what he offered in sermons and counseling sessions had little power to transform the inner character of the people. "They were starving for a word from God," Richard recalls, "and I had nothing to give them. Nothing. I was spiritually bankrupt, and I knew it."[52]

The Bible Richard was using when he wrote *Celebration of Discipline*.

Desperate, Richard turned to the devotional masters of the Christian faith whose writings he had been exposed to in college. Reading their words with new eyes, Richard saw that their relationship to Jesus as the defining reality of their lives had infused them with a flaming vision of God, enabling them to stay grounded when everything around them was in chaos.

It hardly mattered which ancient writer he read in those days—Brother Lawrence's *The Practice of the Presence of God*, Teresa of Avila's *Interior Castle*, John Woolman's *Journal*—they all knew God in ways far beyond anything Richard had ever experienced. What he read settled him, deepened him. Soaking in the stories of people who were aflame with the fire of divine love developed in him a deep desire to live this kind of life.

The second major influence was meeting Dr. Dallas Willard. When the Fosters arrived at the Woodlake church, Dallas, Jane, and their two children, John and Becky, were already there. A respected philosophy professor at the University of Southern California and an ordained Baptist pastor, Dallas was well-versed in the spiritual classics and an avid student of scripture. He served as the church's worship leader and teacher of adult education, communicating a compelling vision for where and how God is active in the nitty gritty of everyday life.

Soon the Willards and Fosters were in each other's homes, learning together, laughing together, weeping together, praying together. And always, Richard recalls, always there was a wonderful sense of God's abiding presence.

A third formative influence came through a Lutheran pastor named William Vaswig. When Richard met Bill at a gathering of local pastors, he recognized him at once as a person who thirsted for the deeper things of God. Richard took Vaswig aside to say, "You know more about prayer than I do. Would you teach me everything you know?" Bill agreed so long as they actually *prayed*—"a lively, honest, heartfelt, soul-searching, hilarious praying."

As Richard and Bill's prayer sessions began to take on the feel and character of the experiences Richard was reading about in the devotional masters, he shared his enthusiasm with Beth Shapiro, head of the elder board at the Woodlake church. A registered nurse, Beth began stopping by the church after her night shift at the hospital ended to spend an hour or two praying with Richard. Whomever and whatever—people in the congregation or people outside the congregation—Beth and Richard prayed for them. Beth asked God to give her patients at the hospital the gift of restored health and well-being. The stories of God's divine intervention were multiplying.

These three influences converged in those early days to promote a quiet revolution in Richard Foster's heart and mind. He was learning about the surrounding reality of God's eternal Kingdom, the function of prayer in a believer's life, and the power of spiritual Disciplines to align our will with the will of God. These experiences provided the depth and the substance he needed personally and the depth and substance that his congregation desperately needed.

While resources on the spiritual Disciplines abound today, in the early 1970s, this was not the case. Richard Foster, Dallas Willard, Bill Vaswig, and Beth Shapiro were plowing uncultivated ground, learning about spiritual practices that many Protestant evangelicals either viewed with apprehension or simply had not tried.

As Richard shared what he was learning with the Woodlake congregation, he witnessed mounting evidence of profound spiritual growth and transformation in the people he served. The fledgling believers under his care were developing and maturing into the character of Christ.

In the excitement of discovery and spiritual confirmation, Richard sensed that they were onto something of enormous significance. Perhaps some of the things they were learning could be of help to others—providing the "rope" so desperately needed to help Christians successfully navigate the unrelenting storms of change. But with his energy so tightly focused on the needs of his congregation, Richard hadn't the time to write a single word about any of it.

This was about to change. It was time for Ron Woodward to come back into his life.

LAND OF MILK AND HONEY

One day Woodward telephoned
with a surprising invitation. He invited Richard to consider joining
him at Newberg Friends Church in
Oregon as part of a pastoral team.
This arrangement, Woodward explained, would give Richard the
space and time to develop his thinking about spiritual formation into
Christlikeness and do some writing.

Ron Woodward

Richard prayed about the opportunity, discussed it with his wife,
Carolynn, with Dallas Willard and
Bill Vaswig, and discerned that the
invitation was indeed of God. The
year was 1974. Richard, Carolynn, and their sons, Joel and
Nathan, packed their belongings and headed north. Richard's
formative years in the desert were complete.

Once established in Newberg, Richard meditated on the
life of Jesus and reread the devotional masters. He developed
a list of spiritual Disciplines that they all held in common. "I
had been doing many of these things from my earliest days, but
I didn't have them clear in my mind; I had never quite understood what was going on spiritually. The practice of a Discipline
can be very beneficial without our knowing what it is all about,
but when we have a sense of what God is doing with us, it takes
on even greater significance."[53]

Richard invited the Newberg congregation to join him in
study and practice of the Disciplines. He selected twelve disciplines that could be practiced by people living busy lives—
young mothers raising children, building contractors, people in
business, medical personnel, teachers—and published articles
about their shared experience. As Richard's thinking clarified,
he developed a tentative outline for a book. In March of 1977,

Richard registered for the Warner Pacific Writers' Conference because it promised attendees fifteen minutes with a publisher.

When Richard met with Roy M. Carlisle from Harper & Row, he handed him a book outline divided into three sections: The Inward Disciplines (meditation, prayer, fasting, study), The Outward Disciplines (simplicity, solitude, submission, service), and The Corporate Disciplines (confession, worship, guidance, celebration). "This book," Richard explained, "will be for all those who are disillusioned by the superficialities of modern culture, including modern religious culture, and are looking for a way to move beyond surface living into the depths of intimate fellowship with God."

Intrigued, Carlisle asked to know where the idea came from. "The idea for this book did not come out of any particular fascination with classical Disciplines or intellectual interest in spirituality," Richard explained. "It really came out of desperation. In my first church, I was with a wonderful group of people who really wanted God. I began to see that many of the great devotional masters of the past had something to say that could actually set people free. And so we began to study and experiment with the Disciplines to see what could happen. We saw people substantially helped: people were set free from ingrained habit patterns that had held them down for many years."[54] This book, Richard asserted, is what is needed to guide followers of Jesus through the current maelstrom of change.

Listening to Richard, it was clear to Carlisle that the young author had thoroughly researched his subject and was, himself, an experienced practitioner. When Richard assured him that he could write the book fairly quickly, Carlisle felt inclined to give it a go.

"When I returned to Harper's office in San Francisco and presented Richard Foster's proposal to our editorial board, I was met with resistance," Carlisle recalls. "No one thought that evangelicals would read a book written by a Quaker pastor with the 'Roman Catholic' spiritual Disciplines as the topic." But Richard Lucas, Director of Marketing at Harper, and a former

Jesuit priest, urged Clayton Carlton and the publication board to take a risk—to give Richard full latitude in his writing. Of the hundreds of unsolicited manuscripts and proposals the editors at Harper & Row received that year, Richard's was one of the few they accepted.

With a green light from Harper, the Newberg pastoral team committed to cover Richard's pastoral duties. This freed him to pen in longhand on a yellow pad the thirteen chapters of *Celebration of Discipline* in just thirty days.

Two friends assisted with the project. Mary Myton typed the chapters, and Bess Bulgin, a published poet, offered helpful suggestions about wording. Richard acknowledged their valuable assistance in the introduction, stating that "books are best written in community."

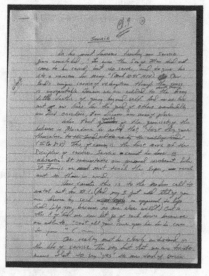

This hand-written page is from the original yellow pad manuscript.

Once the final manuscript was delivered, Harper accepted it as written, with only a slight alteration in the title. They substituted "liberation" with "celebration."

Arguably, Harper & Row took a risk in publishing *Celebration of Discipline*. Roy Carlisle maintains that had the book been published ten years earlier, "It would have dropped in a hole and disappeared." But now, arriving just when it did, *Celebration of Discipline* felt like an answer to prayer. It provided the practical spiritual guidance people needed to safely traverse a rapidly transitioning landscape. No doubt this is why the book received such an enthusiastic reception.

The first royalty check Richard received
from Harper and Row!

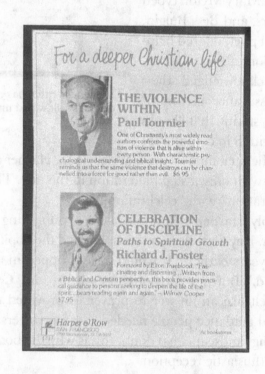

— PART II —

Reception

*My primary concern as a writer is not so much to be accepted,
but rather to express myself honestly. When I have done so,
the rest lies with God.*[55]

Martin Luther King Jr. declared, "Set yourself earnestly to discover what you are made to do and then give yourself passionately to the doing of it." *Celebration of Discipline* was Richard Foster's response to King's clarion call. The book defined what human beings are made to do and offered a time-tested and reliable way to engage. It took time, however, for word to get around that a resource was available that delivered on its promise of personal transformation. This was accomplished, in large part, through the focused effort of individuals like David Leach.

David met Richard Foster at a Quaker pastor's conference shortly after the book was published. His conversation with Richard during a long walk on the beach inspired David to read the book. What he read captured his imagination. Convinced that *Celebration of Discipline* possessed the capacity to bring revival to the entire church, David purchased multiple cases of the book to distribute in his travels as the executive director of Friends

Marriage Encounter. He gave every pastor and Christian leader he encountered their own personal copy, including John, a staff worker with Youth for Christ.[56]

In 2018 John attended the event at George Fox University honoring the fortieth anniversary of *Celebration of Discipline*. When John learned that members of the Leach family were present, he tracked them down. He had brought with him the first edition copy that David Leach had inscribed for him all those years before. Showing them the book, John conveyed his profound gratitude for the gift that had shaped his life with God.[57]

Enthusiastic individuals like David Leach were among the first to promote *Celebration of Discipline*. The first group to recognize and commend the book's singular contribution was Richard Foster's own peers. At the 1978 Christian Writers Conference, a national board of authors and editors named him "Writer of the Year for Nonfiction."

As *Celebration of Discipline* became more widely read, however, it elicited mixed reviews. In a culture inundated by fads and self-help schemes, the book's promise of transformation in the character of Christ was met with tight-lipped skepticism. Among Protestant evangelicals, a handful of leaders already alarmed by the growing interest in subjective spiritual experience published harsh reviews denouncing the book—it was too Catholic, it was New Age, it was "a perfidious espousal of works-righteousness."[58]

How did Richard respond to his critics? While he took them seriously, as seen in the 1988 "revised and expanded" edition of the book, Richard's research and personal experience had convinced him of the efficacy of the spiritual practices. He wrote *Celebration of Discipline* to convey in contemporary terms the consensus that Christians throughout the ages had understood about the spiritual Disciplines as practiced by disciples of Jesus Christ. His intent was to share the good news of his discovery, not to defend that discovery, which is what enabled him to field objections with such remarkable equanimity.

"I had a deep feeling when the manuscript was completed, that I had done what I was meant to do. It's not my part to sell it. And strangely, the published book seems to have an existence entirely apart from me."[59]

The mixed reception of the book underscores just how unusual *Celebration of Discipline* was in the publishing world of the late seventies. No one was writing about ancient spiritual practices, and it was a real question whether there would be a market for such a book. How did it happen?

CHAPTER 4

An Unexpected Opportunity

It is one thing to write a book. It is quite another to have your manuscript picked up by a top-level publisher. How did an unknown, first-time author receive this rare opportunity? To answer that question, we need to know something about Harper & Row.

TAKING A FLY

Spiritually-based publishing had been a constant theme within Harper's program since its founding in 1817. In 1977, when it became clear that most readers of religious books were located west of the Mississippi, Senior Vice President and Publisher Clayton E. Carlson moved from New York to the California Bay Area to become the director for the newly formed HarperSanFrancisco. Carlson proceeded to hire three editors, a denominational editor, a Catholic editor, and an evangelical editor. His choice for evangelical editor was Roy M. Carlisle whom he hired in 1976 because, as Carlson put it, "Carlisle knew booksellers and was acquainted with people who 'did religion as a business.'" After a couple of years learning the editorial trade, Carlson sent Carlisle

Roy M. Carlisle

out on the road to find new authors who had something to say.

When Carlisle met Richard Foster at the writer's conference, he saw at once that Richard fit the bill. Not only was Carlisle drawn professionally to the enthusiastic thirty-six-year-old author, but he felt personally drawn as well. Carlisle brought Richard's proposal back to Clayton Carlson and the publication board at HarperSanFrancisco. At the time, Carlson recalls, certain kinds of the same books were repeatedly being published. In this context, *Celebration of Discipline* stood out. "It introduced a language and direction forward that sent a chill down my spine," Carlson recalls. "But you cannot predict in advance how an unusual book will do."

Fortunately, Winthrop Knowlton, the former undersecretary of Treasury and current CEO of HarperCollins, was famous for encouraging his senior directors to publish unconventional books helping readers understand shifts in the culture and what to do about them. "So," Carlson says, "I thought why not?" With the support of Roy Carlisle and Richard Lucas, Carlson decided to "take a fly" and publish. Sales were slow that first year, and the marketing team worried that the book might not break out, but then it did, proving Carlson's instincts right. *Celebration of Discipline* became a bestseller.

Harper's publication of *Celebration of Discipline* had an unexpected second effect. In an interview, Richard recalled, "Some publishers feel that *Celebration* marked a turning point in the publishing world toward literature with a deep interest in spirituality, personal transformation, and learning to walk with God."[60] The public reception of *Celebration of Discipline* did, in fact, initiate a shift in the Christian publishing industry, as

Phyllis Tickle noted, away from books emphasizing behavior to those focusing on the inner life.

Addressing authors at a writer's conference, Roy Carlisle explained that there are basically three kinds of books: books written by thought leaders, books interpreting the contribution of thought leaders, and curriculum making the thought leaders' ideas accessible. There is no question, Carlisle said, that Richard Foster was—and is—a thought leader.

Carlisle recalls, "*Celebration of Discipline* became a huge bestseller sparking a movement toward deeper spiritual practices like no other book of its time. What startled everyone was that it sold to Catholics, Christian conservatives, and mainline Protestants, metabolizing Catholic spiritual Disciplines and Quaker devotional materials into language that appealed to all people of faith. This was a phenomenon. No religious book publisher today could even imagine not publishing books on deeper spirituality for any believer, so this shift has crossed all lines."[61]

It took courage for Clayton Carlson to publish a guide for the inner journey that would either be an abysmal flop or a great success, but this was part of Harper's innovative agenda. When Carlson instructed Carlisle to watch for books that possessed the potential to start a movement, Carlisle brought him *Celebration of Discipline*. It was the right decision at the right time, one that the publisher never regretted.

RAMPAGING AWAY

Shortly after the book was released in America, Harper sent a copy of *Celebration of Discipline* to Edward England who was in charge of new publications for Hodder & Stoughton in the UK. England read the book and urged his team, despite the unknown author, to "take a punt" on publishing a paperback edition. Tony Collins managed the project, agreeing with England that the book "opened up doors of spiritual growth which we had heard of but knew little about."[62]

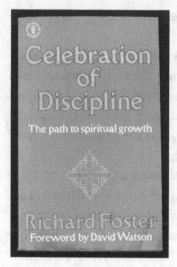

Celebration of Discipline took off at once in the UK, rapidly becoming a bestseller. "The book rampaged away," recalls Collins, "garnering widespread positive reviews and creating an entire new awareness in the evangelical churches of the UK that there was more in our faith than we had suspected."

The editor at Hodder & Stoughton, who worked directly with Richard Foster in the promotion of his subsequent books, was Carolyn Armitage Scriven. She described *Celebration of Discipline* as a "game changer" that "rapidly became the 'must read' of the time and was one of the books I was delighted to see go into many editions."

Scriven confides that *Celebration of Discipline* became a companion in her own spiritual journey and a resource to which she regularly returns because "the practice of the Disciplines is the practice of seeking and coming into the presence of God, something which occupies a lifetime and not just a season."[63]

Dallas Willard remarked, "Everywhere I go I meet those whose lives have been changed encountering the book. *Celebration of Discipline* has quietly asserted itself in the lives of multitudes around the globe and has taken its place as a guide to the uplands of the spiritual life for the late twentieth century. It places us on the path of life with those who have succeeded in walking with Jesus in every circumstance and shows us accessible patterns of action through which interaction with his Kingdom is assured to us. This is the secret of its power. If you wish to know in yourself the reality of the gracious life of God seen in the Bible, you may find no better guide than *Celebration of Discipline*."[64]

Commenting on soaring sales in the United States and abroad, Richard Foster observed, *"Celebration of Discipline* has taken on a life of its own. The book has sold because of its content rather than some big name. Things are happening here that are not under my control; it is not my book. It belongs to the people of God. My business is to do what I feel I have been asked to do and let the results rest with God. Let's pray that the benefit will be found in seeing the goodness of the Kingdom of God being more and more manifested in the lives of people."[65]

Any book biography worth its salt includes data detailing speaking requests, sales figures, subsequent editions, endorsements, and book reviews. So, buckle your seat belt, here we go!

RICHARD FOSTER

Newberg Pastor Writer-Of-Year

CHAPTER 5

By the Numbers

"*Celebration of Discipline* has sold over 350,000 copies since first published in 1978 and shows no signs of slowing," observed a Fuller Bookstore reviewer in 1989. "Indeed, it has become a contemporary classic as it has met a continual need in the Christian community. It has pointed a way beyond the superficiality to which we abhorrently cling."[66]

A year following publication, invitations from forty-one of the fifty states in the US poured in for Richard Foster to lecture on the concepts contained in *Celebration of Discipline*. By 1980, *Celebration of Discipline* was growing steadily in breadth of readership and influence. Harper editor Roy Carlisle attributed the spike in sales to several influences: the timely release of the book, positive book reviews, published citations, word-of-mouth promotion, Richard's personal interviews and radio spots, and his energetic speaking schedule.

On nine different occasions, the esteemed Staley Distinguished Christian Scholar Lecture Program funded Richard's speaking engagements at various colleges and universities. Within a period of several years, Richard received speaking invitations from fifty-seven colleges and universities, twenty-one seminaries, eight Christian parachurch organizations, several missionary organizations, and Christian bookseller conventions.

It was clear that *Celebration of Discipline* had taken a firm hold in the minds and imaginations of Christians across North America, Puerto Rico, Central and South America. As invitations began to arrive from England, Germany, Australia, Hong Kong, China, Korea, South Africa, and Costa Rica, Harper & Row was kept busy granting permission for the text to be translated.

It was Harper & Row's custom to print 5,000 to 7,000 copies of a title at a time. Within two years, *Celebration* had climbed to number four on *Bookstore Journal's* annual list of bestsellers, initiating a reprint. By 1981, *Christian Booksellers, Bookstore Journal,* and *Better Book Room Best Sellers* ranked it at number four. When *Pulpit Helps* surveyed its readers in 1982 to discover their "Top Ten" picks, *Celebration of Discipline* was listed as number one. By then, *Celebration of Discipline* was in its fifteenth printing. Booksellers associated with the Evangelical Christian Publishers Association ranked the book that same year among the top ten bestselling books in their bookstores.

The book has been on Christian Book Distributors annual bestselling list since 1980. In 2000, *The Christian Century* listed *Celebration* as number one of HarperSanFrancisco's bestselling publications. By the second decade of the twenty-first century, *Celebration of Discipline* had sold well over two million copies and been translated into twenty-eight different languages. The spiritual classic remains on the short list of Harper's all-time top-selling books on Christian spirituality.

SUBSEQUENT EDITIONS

In 1988, HarperCollins marked the tenth anniversary with a "revised and expanded" edition of *Celebration of Discipline.* This was unusual, as the text of subsequent editions normally was unchanged.

Curious to know what specific revisions had been made, I conducted a line-by-line comparison of the 1978 and 1988 editions. While the basic message remained unchanged, I saw that in the later edition, Richard had taken the opportunity to expand his discussion of the inner Discipline of prayer, the outer Discipline of simplicity, and the corporate Discipline of celebration. The chapter receiving the most revision was the inner Discipline of meditation. Having discovered that his readers were, by and large, unfamiliar with the long tradition of biblical meditation, the opening chapter received a wholesale revision (more will be said about this later).

When HarperCollins invited leading clergy, theologians, politicians, and authors to submit endorsements for the tenth anniversary edition, Mark Hatfield, a United States senator from Oregon, observed that heeding the call to follow Jesus in the midst of a culture that ignores Christ and embraces materialism is exceedingly difficult and can easily lead to frustration and defeat. He praised *Celebration of Discipline* for "helping believers to know and follow the Savior in contemporary society."[67]

Lewis B. Smedes, professor of ethics at Fuller Theological Seminary, supported Hatfield's assessment. *"Celebration of Discipline* has brought precious new meaning to the living of the Christian life in our sated world."[68] Madeleine L'Engle, author of *A Wrinkle in Time*, added, *"Celebration of Discipline* won me when it was first published, a fresh voice of reality . . . and there is even more need of Richard Foster's wisdom today. If everybody in this country would read—and heed—this book, what a difference it would make to the planet—nay, to the cosmos."[69]

In 1998, HarperCollins honored the book's twentieth anniversary by publishing a third (unrevised) edition of *Celebration of Discipline*. Twenty years later, HarperOne published a fourth edition heralding forty years of stellar achievement. Each subsequent edition included a fresh foreword by Richard Foster; the fortieth anniversary edition featured the addition of two new essays and an annotated bibliography of books from the fourth to the twenty-first centuries that have "inspired, informed, and grounded Christians during periods of unprecedented change."[70]

All of Harper's published editions of *Celebration of Discipline*.

Reviewers praised the book's forty-year history of offering practical guidance to Christians seeking a closer communion with God, more loving relationships with others, and a community life that celebrates God's great gift to us. "Richard Foster knows the fullness of the Spirit in his own life and he values highly the ancient Disciplines of [people] of faith down the years. What is more, he has obviously worked at them himself. The book shows us clear ways that we can incorporate these Disciplines into our daily activities, liberating us from the 'stifling slavery of self-interest and fear.'"[71] Lee Abbey's *Rapport* declared, "*Celebration of Discipline* by Richard Foster is very popular on both sides of the Atlantic and is well worth the reputation it has gained."[72]

Over time, classics like *Celebration of Discipline* take on a life of their own. Or, more accurately, they take on several million lives as the book intersects with the actual experiences of its readers. Behind the soaring sales were scores of individual stories of personal transformation, of substantive change. What follows are the stories behind the numbers.

CHAPTER 6

The Stories Behind
the Numbers

When Richard Foster sat down to pen *Celebration of Discipline* on a yellow pad, he was careful to use examples that would be as relevant in one hundred years as they were when written. Even as the Disciplines he described were rooted in the spiritual practices of Jesus and the early church, Richard wanted Christians one hundred years into the future to find his book as timeless and reliable as the ancient guidance of the devotional masters had been for him.

Arguably, Richard succeeded in meeting that commitment. When writer Anna Bolch picked up a used copy of the third edition of *Celebration of Discipline*, she wondered if the book would still be relevant to her life and circumstances. Not only did Bolch find it pertinent, but her worn copy became a foundational spiritual resource. The book's teaching of the ancient Disciplines combined with an honest look at contemporary Christian life in a way that helped her to recognize the thread of the Spirit at work in her own life.[73]

Pastor Jamie Buckingham was introduced to *Celebration of Discipline* by a Catholic priest in the Republic of Panama. When he experienced the positive effects of the Disciplines, Buckingham made *Celebration of Discipline* mandatory reading for his church staff. "I am deeply indebted to Richard Foster for clearly defining on paper those things about which the Holy Spirit had already been tugging at my heart."[74]

As pastors recommended *Celebration of Discipline* to their congregations, the readership quickly expanded. Helen Washington, a physical therapist at the Mayo Clinic, found a copy in her church library and read it straight through. "It literally changed my life! It was like water to a very parched soul!"[75]

Pastor Wayne Kofink read *Celebration of Discipline* during a bleak period in his ministry. "I am grateful to Richard Foster for sharing the Disciplines. They helped him and his Woodlake congregation to navigate a difficult passage and they have done the same for us."[76] Pastor Michael Rogers, shared a similar story. "I was working hard, joylessly striving to live out the expectations of my role when I discovered *Celebration of Discipline* and learned I had convoluted grace. I am still a pastor today because of this book."[77]

Author Judith Lechman experienced a similar relief when she read *Celebration of Discipline*. "Much like an old and dear friend, the book helps me to walk steadfastly—even through the bleakest of moments—along the path toward wholeness and God."[78] Barbara Bliss confides, "There have been many storms in my life. But the foundation built brick-by-brick through my practice of the Disciplines has stabilized me. I am stronger today than ever."[79]

Wendy Palmer and Chris Simpson read *Celebration of Discipline* the same year that they became Christians. From the start, the Disciplines guided both of them in their pursuit of God and personal holiness.[80] Simpson says that Richard's introduction to the devotional masters opened doors to him that he had not known were closed. What surprised him the most was learning how passionate God is to know us personally.[81] Connie Pittman had a similar response. *"Celebration of Discipline* introduced me to a new love. As I read and reread the book, it continued to draw me ever deeper into intimacy with God."[82]

Catholic author and monastic Macrina Wiederkehr credits *Celebration of Discipline* for reconnecting her with truths she knew but kept forgetting. "Each Discipline in the book hands me a *tool* that can be useful in helping me to grow in intimacy with God and integrate my inner and outer lives."[90] "As an indulgent people in a selfish age," David McKenna observes, "we do not ordinarily view life in this way or 'celebrate' discipline. But that is the Spirit-guided genius of *Celebration of Discipline*. Out of his own faith and practice, Foster shows us what we are missing— the fullness of life promised by Christ."[83]

McKenna identifies what author and poet Luci Shaw appreciates most about the book. "Where cheap and tawdry values shape society, *Celebration of Discipline* holds up for us a model that is both solid and costly. Here the spiritual life of Christ is fused with the physical; the word is again made flesh; heaven and earth are joined."[84] "Yes!" agrees writer Beth Ratzlaff. "Our practice of the spiritual Disciplines opens a deep channel for the Holy Spirit to flow through as the Spirit recreates souls."[85]

Andy Sloan was introduced to the spiritual Disciplines in the mid-1980s through his reading of *Celebration of Discipline*. The book helped him to "put flesh on the bones of his spiritual life" by providing both form and direction to his commitment to faithfully live the gospel imperative for equity and magnanimity among all peoples.[86]

Janie Robert was working at an orphanage in Zimbabwe when she first read *Celebration of Discipline*. When she travels, she takes along two books: the Bible and that original copy of *Celebration of Discipline*.[87] Grace Ju Miller, dean of the School of Natural and Applied Sciences at Taylor University, does the same. "God has used *Celebration of Discipline* to form me and my students. I carry it with me as I travel the world."[88]

Pastors, educators, healthcare workers, and politicians credit *Celebration of Discipline* for its formative influence in their walk with God and life work. In an era where issues of social justice are inspiring a new generation of Christian leaders, practice of the Disciplines is helping to shape the movement for racial reform.

TRANSFORMATION TAKES ACTION

Leighton Ford was an early advocate for social justice. Over time he noticed that his passion for the work was beginning to take precedence over his personal relationship with God. *Celebration of Discipline* reconnected Ford to the roots of his faith. "No other book apart from the Bible has been so helpful to me in the nurturing of my inward journey of prayer and spiritual growth. This vast mission can never be accomplished apart from a deep rootage in Christ, instructed by the Word of God and nurtured by his Spirit."[89]

Tony Campolo, professor emeritus at Eastern University, tells a similar story. "As an activist, I've had a tendency to get so involved in my 'good works' that I neglect the spiritual Disciplines which keep me in touch with the source of my strength and vision. *Celebration of Discipline* has been a major help in moving me in the direction I want to go."[90]

Lisa Sharon Harper, activist and founder of Freedom Road, also credits *Celebration of Discipline* for helping her to remain rooted in Christ and centered in Christian values. "In the movement for racial healing, we confront the forces of evil in the heavenlies that become visible in the battle for justice on the streets, in board rooms, and across social media. When facing off against powers intent on crushing the image of God on earth, the Disciplines keep me closely connected to Jesus, to the Spirit, and to Scripture, which reminds me of what is true and beautiful in the world. In an era of rapid social transition, the Disciplines ground us in God as they did our spiritual ancestors before us. Rooted in God, as I resist racial injustice, I feel God's smile. To shirk the spiritual Disciplines is to put ourselves and our Kingdom work in peril."[91]

"The desperate need today is not for a greater number of intelligent people, or gifted people, but for deep people," declares *Celebration of Discipline*. "The classical Disciplines of the spiritual life call us to move beyond surface living into the depths. They urge us to be the answer to a hollow world."[92] In *Streams of Living Water,* Richard adds, "The power to be the kind of people we were created to be and the power to do the works of God upon the earth places us on solid ground to engage the demands of the social arena. And no place is in greater need of people full of the Holy Spirit and divine love."[93]

Celebration of Discipline was Renovaré board member Tina Dyer's first introduction to the Disciplines of a well-formed life and God's call to "engage the demands of the social arena." Citing *Celebration of Discipline*'s assertion that "service to be service, must take form and shape in the world in which we live,"[94] Dyer sees that, just like every other part of our identity and life experiences, we cannot be spiritually mature and refuse to see race as a part of our cultural formation that needs reform. "The current urgent business of Christians deeply formed in Christlikeness are the injustices of a racialized culture."

Dyer puts this conviction into action by engaging three specific personal practices. 1) *The Discipline to See.* Dyer asks the Holy Spirit to open her eyes to the world in ways that have been previously invisible. 2) *The Discipline to be Present.* Dyer deliberately goes to places outside of her normal environment to sit with and listen to people who experience the world differently than she. 3) *The Discipline to Act.* As the Spirit leads, Dyer obeys promptings to love and serve the other as would Jesus in her place.

FORMATION OPENS THE APERTURE

Engagement in the social arena is an important area of growth for me because it was not part of my early formation. Growing up, I had very little exposure to people from other groups, cultures, or ethnicities. As a consequence, my vision was limited. I leaned hard into the practices described in *Celebration of Discipline* as a way to nurture my personal formation in Christlikeness. And when I became a pastor, I worked hard to foster an atmosphere of corporate formation in our church community. But my attention did not venture far from our local context. That changed when Jesus opened the aperture of my heart to let in the world.

My ministry colleague approached me one day to share her sense that God might want us to travel to Rwanda with World Vision. She explained that we would meet with Christian brothers and sisters who had survived the 1994 genocide and explore ways we might partner to assist their healing and recovery.

I was perfectly willing for my colleague to go, representing our church, but resisted her insistence that I come along. The reason? I was afraid. I was afraid of going to a place that was unfamiliar to be among a people whose suffering runs deep. I could not see how I—or our church—could make any substantive difference. I did not want to go.

Talking this over with Jesus, I agreed, at least, to read about conditions in Rwanda—a small country reeling from the triple storm of genocide, AIDS, and poverty. It soon became clear that Jesus wanted both of us to make the trip. I reluctantly agreed but remained anxious because I didn't know what to expect. During the long flight to East Africa, I gazed down at the huge expanse of the Sahara Desert and muttered, "What am I doing here? This is a bad idea." I was surprised to hear Jesus respond, "I am eager for you to meet some of my dearest friends."

Celebration of Discipline maintains that "true service builds community."[95] Before Jesus opened the aperture of my heart, my vision for spiritual transformation in Christ was limited to what I could imagine. Our visit became the first of many trips taken by members of our congregation and me to Rwanda. We developed cherished friendships with our African brothers and sisters, and our church sponsored hundreds of vulnerable children and their families through World Vision. It was beautiful. It was life changing. And once begun, the effect was continuous.

My experience in Rwanda opened the aperture of my heart to develop relationships with people in my own local community whose lives and experience differ significantly from my own. In the words of Tina Dyer, "As Christ is fully formed in us, we will be a people who can see, who can hear, who can understand and be glad to be with others, especially the Othered, and act for the good of the Kingdom."[96]

CHAPTER 7

Storm Clouds Gather:
Critiques

While *Celebration of Discipline* was warmly welcomed in many
circles, it did have its detractors. The most sustained criticism
came from evangelical Protestants. To understand their perspective and specific objections, it is helpful to review the nature
of evangelical spirituality as summarized by Evan Howard, author and professor at Fuller Theological Seminary.

The first characteristic of evangelical spirituality is
its protest against Catholicism. Its reaction against
Catholic "mystical consciousness" would make it difficult to appreciate contemplation and/or meditation
since in the Catholic scheme contemplation is part of
mystical prayer.

Second, evangelical spirituality is marked more by
doing than resting. Its activism tends to preclude spiritual "passivity," associated with the posture of meditation and/or contemplation.

Third, evangelical spirituality affirms the pri-
macy of the written Word. Evangelicals are more

comfortable with spiritual practices involving the use of the intellect rather than the imagination. Discursive meditation is preferred over imaginative mediation of the Ignatian type.[97]

A fourth characteristic of evangelical spirituality is found in the classic tenet of the Protestant Reformation that we are saved by grace through faith alone. Some critics argued that, as Christ has secured our salvation, there is nothing more to be done, and these critics contended that *Celebration of Discipline* advocates a theology of works righteousness. Richard clarified, "The grace of God *is* unearned and unearnable, but if we ever expect to grow in grace, we must pay the price of a consciously chosen course of action which involves both individual and group life. Spiritual growth is the purpose of the classic Disciplines."[98] But his critics remained unconvinced.

As *Celebration of Discipline* exposed many Protestant evangelicals for the first time to spiritual traditions and practices held by the church for millennia and readers responded with enthusiasm, apologist Dave Hunt, editor and publisher of *Media Spotlight*, T. A. McMahon, Albert James Dager, Dave Nelson, and the Lighthouse Trails Research Project vigorously challenged this. Their published articles and books centered on Richard's promotion of biblical meditation.

It is beyond the scope of this chapter to give a complete response to all the issues that were raised, but two central concerns will be addressed: first, the argument that contemplation/meditation is fundamentally non-Christian in orientation, and second, that the practice cannot be grounded biblically.

In 1985, Dave Hunt and T. A. McMahon co-authored a book titled, *The Seduction of Christianity*. On page 173, they quoted Richard as having said, "We simply must become convinced of the importance of thinking and experiencing in images." Use of the imagination in contemplative prayer or meditation, the authors contended, is associated with psycho-spirituality, a technique employed by occultists to generate an altered state of consciousness. By encouraging the use of imagination, they said Richard and authors like him were "creating a powerful New Age 'paradigm shift' that [was] changing the way thousands of current pastors and future pastors view Christianity and the Bible."[99]

Seven years later, in 1992, Hunt and McMahon launched a newsletter called *The Berean Call*. Behind every article was the commitment to "equip adherents with materials to help them confront and combat every form of contemplative experience."[100]

In 1990 Dave Nelson published an article in "The Shield: A Ministry to Non-Christian Religions and Aberrant Christian Groups," censoring *Celebration of Discipline* for its alleged

1. promotion of transcendental meditation and altered states of consciousness,
2. promotion of a form of visualization that parallels astral travel and sets people up for the possibility of demonic influence,
3. misunderstanding of the dangerous nature of Eastern mystical practices,
4. failure to anchor the twelve practices in scripture,
5. teaching that Christ will personally appear during meditation,
6. failure to "test the spirits" to guarantee the source of our experience.[101]

The Lighthouse Trails Research Project formed in 2002 with a mission "to protect Christians from a contemplative spirituality that is quickly gaining a foothold among evangelical Christians." The project names Richard Foster as "the major figure in bringing contemplative spirituality into the evangelical/Protestant church" and *Celebration of Discipline* as the culprit. "Although Foster may be sincere and well-meaning, he has unfortunately drawn on [Buddhist] tradition that the Bible does not present or condone."[102]

In the 1988 "revised and expanded" edition of *Celebration of Discipline*, Richard responded to these concerns by inserting guidelines for the practice of meditation, warning readers against the possible distortions and abuses of contemplation. In subsequent publications, Richard reinforced this caution. In *Prayer: Finding the Heart's True Home* (1992), he counseled that the practice of contemplation should be approached carefully and prayerfully, as it takes time for the believer to create a proper biblical foundation and learn the principles of discernment so that they do not fall into error. In *Streams of Living Water* (1998), Richard devoted four pages to the "potential perils" of contemplation, reminding readers not to isolate themselves from ordinary life, to beware of excessive asceticism, not to marginalize the intellectual dimension of faith, and not to ignore the necessity of communal life.

The critics, however, chose to ignore Richard's clarifications. In 1992, James Dager published a lengthy article in *The Shield* condemning the 1978 edition for having "fallen into the trap of . . . incorporating unbiblical methodologies and philosophies in its spiritual exercises."[103] Claiming that Richard had simply co-opted Roman Catholic practices, Dager alleged that these had been adapted in the fourth century from paganism and assimilated by the Catholic Church. In the article, Dager went so far as to equate prayerful contemplation of Jesus with occult visualization, warning that this practice opens innocent practitioners to the influence of demonic spirit guides. Blaming Richard's Quaker background for his alleged naivete, Dager charged that "Quakerism is close to Buddhism in its philosophical understanding of God."[104]

Elliot Miller, editor in chief of *Christian Research Journal*, read Dager's article in *The Shield*. In the following issue, he published a letter to the editor cautioning Dager "to avoid the oversimplification and other logical fallacies that often characterize Dave Hunt's approach."[105]

Richard responded to Dager's public allegations in a personal letter. Richard identified the canon of scripture as the source for his chapter on meditation with the intended outcome being transformation into the character of Jesus Christ. Richard informed Dager that even a cursory review of Quaker writings will quickly dispel any thought that Quakers and Buddhists share "a common philosophical understanding of God." Dager did not choose to respond.

In a subsequent interview with the *Wichita Eagle*, Richard elaborated, "Until the rise of rationalism, meditation was listed among the classic Disciplines of the spiritual life. But with the emergence of the scientific age in the mid-1800s, anything that wasn't cerebral or empirical was viewed by evangelical Protestants with suspicion. In the 1960s, people who had become disillusioned and dissatisfied with cerebral religion were drawn to experiential faith. Experiential faith is not anti-rational, neither does it limit one's faith to the empirical. Meditation, like the other classic Disciplines of the Christian life, is simply a way of coming into touch with God, a way of setting oneself before God so that God can work the needed inner transformation of heart."[106]

Setting the Record Straight

It was not long before Christian scholars, theologians, and clergy joined the conversation, framing *Celebration of Discipline* in the broad context of church history.

When Dr. Craig Blomberg of Denver Theological Seminary read Dave Nelson's critique of *Celebration of Discipline* in *The Shield*, in the following issue he published a rebuttal. Noting that Nelson's concerns primarily addressed Richard's treatment of meditation, Blomberg clarified that meditation is sourced not in Eastern mystical tradition but in the actual practices of Jesus Christ and the time-tested practice of Christian history's most godly people.

"Foster has categorically denied promoting Zen, yoga, transcendental meditation, or any Eastern mystical practice which might result in an altered state of consciousness. The spiritual practices that *Celebration of Discipline* promotes do not produce abnormal states of consciousness, but rather allow a simple detachment from the normal distractions of life which hinder our communion with Christ." By omitting discussion of Richard's chapter on the Discipline of study, Blomberg continued, Nelson categorically misrepresented Richard's meaning regarding encounters with the living Christ. Imagining yourself as being present during the events of the gospel narratives is much like picturing Jesus sitting in a chair in a room conversing with a person praying to him there. It simply is a tool to make the reality of Christ's presence with us more vivid.

Blomberg proceeded to present solid biblical precedent for the practice of Christian contemplation.

- The experience of Moses (Deuteronomy 34:10) and Elijah (I Kings 19:12–14).
- Examples found in the book of Psalms (cf. Psalm 27, 42, 73, 131).
- The New Testament emphasis on the contemplative life:
  - Mary "treasured all these things and pondered them in her heart" (Luke 2:19).
  - In John chapters 14–17. Jesus prays that we may participate with him in the intimacy and enjoyment of divine love (John 14:23; 17:21, 24–26).
- The apostle Paul describes his mystical experience of having been taken up into the third heaven (2 Corinthians 12:1–4).
- Other New Testament references include Luke 10:39, 42; Acts 7:54–56; 2 Corinthians 3:18; and Hebrews 12:2.

Blomberg concluded, "*Celebration of Discipline* represents rich, biblical teaching on topics that American Christians desperately need to recover."[107]

Dr. Tom Schwanda of Wheaton College shared Blomberg's assessment. In a chapter Schwanda wrote for *Embracing Contemplation: Reclaiming a Spiritual Practice*, he states that more than anyone else, Richard Foster has been unfairly attacked by evangelicals for his promotion of Christian contemplation. The specific allegations leveled against the Discipline of meditation reflect an ignorance of scriptural precedent and over two thousand years of Christian spiritual practice.[108]

Dallas Willard concurs. "The complaint that imaginative meditative techniques such as Foster describes in *Celebration of Discipline* are contrary to Scripture and are 'merely human,' or even involve cooperation with Satan or evil spirits is simply false." Meditation as a Discipline has been practiced in Judaism from the start, as evidenced by multiple examples in the Old Testament, in the book of Psalms, and in the New Testament.[109]

Todd Hunter, bishop in the Anglican Church in North America, asserts that the common thread uniting the detractors is a general disdain for anything even remotely comparable to Roman Catholic spiritual practices. For Protestant evangelicals, you pray the sinner's prayer and go to heaven; there is no vision for inner transformation into the character of Jesus. "But *Celebration of Discipline* presents a historic perspective of the way that both Eastern and Western churches have embraced the goodness and power of the spiritual Disciplines, encouraging followers of Jesus to see that these are not exclusively Catholic practices but Disciplines essential to spiritual formation in the character of Jesus."[110]

In *Dynamics of Spiritual Life: An Evangelical Theology of Renewal*, theologian Richard Lovelace agrees that, on the whole, evangelicals have mislaid the Protestant tradition of spiritual formation. As contemplative practices have been negated in favor of the active life, "a gap has emerged in contemporary evangelicalism between peoples' expectations in the Christian life and engagement with the in-depth spiritual theology that our Christian forebearers managed to articulate. As a consequence evangelicals who long for a deeper, more intimate life with God remain uncertain of how to proceed."[111]

This may be the current state of the evangelical church, but as we have seen, a review of Christian history reveals that for more than two millennia, devoted Christians have looked to the pattern of Jesus for direction in their life with God. We see that Jesus engaged in a variety of spiritual practices designed to increase his level of receptivity to his heavenly Father (his forty-day fast, withdrawing to solitary places to pray). We witness him meditating on scripture and conversing with God in prayer, through which he received guidance and strength for his public ministry (Mark 1:35–39). "These spiritual practices," asserts Dr. Christopher Hall, "consistently nourished the incarnate Son's relationship with the Father."[112]

In *Celebration of Discipline,* Richard effectively reintroduces modern believers to the Disciplines of Jesus. Approaching each chapter similarly, he first makes the case, then establishes a biblical foundation (quoting from forty-six of the sixty-six books in the Protestant Bible, 108 references to the Gospels alone), appeals to its validity in the modern age, provides quotes from classical writers, and suggests ways to practice each.[113]

— Part III —

Ongoing Transformative Influence

Most books, even those that make a big splash at the time of publication, eventually fade away like the ripples on a pond. Only a relative few take on lives of their own so that they are generating new ripples even a generation later. Far more rare is a book whose life story tells not only of survival into future generations but even of growing vitality.[114] *Celebration of Discipline* ranks as one of the "great spiritual books of our time" if for no other reason than the phenomenon of its continuing life.

When, in December of 1979, Harper & Row listed *Celebration of Discipline* among their top three bestselling books, a journalist from *The Wichita Eagle* asked Richard Foster why he thought the book was selling so well. Richard replied that practice of the classical, spiritual Disciplines—meditation, prayer, fasting, study, simplicity, solitude, submission, service, confession, worship, guidance, and celebration—were helping individuals to break free of superficial habits separating them from God and enabling them to achieve depth in their lives.[115] "Our world cries out for a theology of spiritual growth that has been proven to work in the midst of the harsh realities of daily life."[116]

CHAPTER 8

I See a People

When Richard Foster published *Celebration of Discipline* and readers began reporting stories of significant personal change, it was assumed by many that that individual transformation into Christlikeness would comprise the book's primary contribution. But by the close of the twentieth century, it was apparent that this was not the case. As disciplined followers of Jesus gathered in worship, entire communities of believers were being transformed and carrying that effect out beyond the walls of the church into the world.

Looking on, Richard recognized this as the true legacy of *Celebration of Discipline.* He put what he was shown into words:

God is gathering his people once again, creating of them an all-inclusive community of loving persons with Jesus Christ as the community's prime sustainer and most glorious inhabitant.

This community is breaking forth in multiplied ways and varied forms.

I see it happening, this great new gathering of the people of God.

I see an obedient, disciplined, freely gathered people who know in our day the life and powers of the Kingdom of God.

I see a people of cross and crown, of courageous action and sacrificial love.

I see a people who are combining evangelism with social action, the transcendent Lordship of Jesus with the suffering servant Messiah.

I see a people who are buoyed up by the vision of Christ's everlasting rule, not only imminent on the horizon, but already bursting forth in our midst.

I see a people . . . I see a people . . . even though it feels as if I am peering through a glass darkly.

I see a country pastor from Indiana embracing an urban priest from New Jersey and together praying for the peace of the world. I see a people.

I see a Catholic monk from the hills of Kentucky standing alongside a Baptist evangelist from the streets of Los Angeles and together offering up a sacrifice of praise. I see a people.

I see social activists from the urban centers of Hong Kong joining with Pentecostal preachers from the barrios of Sao Paulo and together weeping over the spiritually lost and the plight of the poor. I see a people.

I see laborers from Soweto and landowners from Pretoria honoring and serving each other out of reverence for Christ. I see a people.

I see Hutu and Tutsi, Serb and Croat, Mongol and Han Chinese, African-American and Anglo, Latino and Native American all sharing and caring and loving one another. I see a people.

I see the sophisticated standing with the simple, the elite standing with the dispossessed, the wealthy standing with the poor. I see a people.

I see a people, I tell you, a people from every race
and nation and tongue and stratum of society, joining
hearts and hands and minds and voices declaring,
  Amazing Grace! How sweet the sound
  That saved a wretch like me!
  I once was lost but now am found,
  Was blind but now I see![117]

NOW—BUT NOT YET

"I see a people," Richard declared, "I see a people . . . even
though it feels as if I am peering through a glass darkly." Now
. . . but not yet. Social commentator Michael Frost doesn't see
it. He compares contemporary Western culture to an airport
departure lounge "full of people who don't belong where they
currently find themselves and whose interactions with others
are fleeting, perfunctory, and trivial." Echoing Richard, Charles
Moore places the solution firmly in the hands of God's people.
"When the church lives out its original calling as a contrast
community and foretaste of God's eternal Kingdom, a new kind
of social existence is possible."[118] Relationships are healed and
lives transformed in the context of authentic biblical community.
This is what being the church is all about.

It is just here that *Celebration of Discipline* was having its greatest impact. Individuals from every race and nation and tongue
and stratum of society were joining hearts and hands and minds
and voices in a shared commitment to go deep in their life with
God.

Richard's vision was slowly coming into focus.

IT BEGINS WITH THE INDIVIDUAL

Christoph Friedrich Blumhardt was among those who investi-
gated the movement. It is important to notice, he said, the order
of transmission. "It is simply not possible to gather hundreds of

people into common fellowship before the members themselves are ready for this. This is especially so if you draw in people who are materialistic, envious, unfree, and unwilling to go the whole way."[119] Charles E. Moore agreed. "If we are honest, we'll recognize that we have been groomed to believe that our lives are ours to do with as we please and that our independence is more important than our involvement in whatever groups we happen to participate in, including the church. We will have to form new lifestyle habits and dispense with old patterns of living and thinking. It will take work. Such a life demands that we engage individually and corporately in very concrete spiritual practices."[120]

James Bryan Smith added a further condition. For it to be contagious, a commitment to spiritual formation must be the lived experience of the pastor. Very little can happen in a church without this. "When a pastor practices the Disciplines, he or she is changed in a way that naturally passes along to the members of his or her congregation."[121]

TONGUES OF FIRE

When I became senior pastor of a church in Golden, Colorado, I was eager to make spiritual formation in Christ our shared purpose. To this end, I enthusiastically shared my experience of the transformative power of the Disciplines in fostering our life with God. I preached through the chapters in *Celebration of Discipline*. We designed congregation-wide experiments for people to "try on" the Disciplines. We offered opportunities for people to gather in small groups to share their experience. My expectation was that this combination of teaching, practice, and sharing would have an immediate metamorphic effect. My optimism was premature.

As *Celebration of Discipline* began to shape our shared vocabulary, not everyone was pleased. Some stoutly resisted our congregation-wide focus on spiritual formation, but many more engaged, initiating a subtle shift in our church culture. A compassionate concern for people suffering from gun violence, hunger, poverty, and homelessness began to emerge. Prayer groups sprang up spontaneously as people researched what was being done and sought direction from the Lord. We partnered with other churches and organizations to pool resources and offer compassionate service. The executive of Denver Presbytery was overheard to say, "the Golden church may be small in size, but their giving and service rivals that of our largest congregations."

Slowly but surely, the principles and practices in *Celebration of Discipline* were taking hold, changing us from the inside out. In time, even some of our more reticent members chose to engage. *Celebration of Discipline* anticipated this, "When the people of God meet together, there often comes a sense of being 'gathered' into one mind, becoming of one accord (Philippians 3:15)."[122] As people felt safe enough to be vulnerable, our gatherings were punctuated by spontaneous breathings of laughter and praise.[123] Trusting Jesus to be present in worship to teach and touch us with his power, the very air felt charged with holy expectancy. Even the way we conducted business changed. Trusting Jesus to guide our decisions, we substituted a deliberate process of corporate discernment for majority rule. My dream that we would become an "all-inclusive community of loving persons with Jesus Christ as our prime sustainer and most glorious inhabitant" was coming to life. It was everything I had hoped for and more.

Scripture assures us that *koinonia*, transformative community, has been God's intent all along. The Bible as a whole provides the source and context, describing not only what has happened in the past but conveying God's prescription for how we can and may live today in the Kingdom of God's rule.[124]

Celebration of Discipline carried the long tradition of Christian spiritual formation like a burning torch into our contemporary setting and set our church on fire.

CHAPTER 9

Fanned into Flame:
The Spiritual Formation Movement

Jesus and his disciples were Middle Eastern Jews whose commitment to spiritual practices and Disciplines was rooted in their faith tradition dating all the way back to God's initial call to Abraham.[125] The practices of silence and solitude, meditation on Scripture, study, prayer, fasting, worship, living simply, generosity, service, and celebration shaped their daily life with God. Following Pentecost, when the Holy Spirit descended to infuse the followers of Jesus with power from on high, they carried the good news of salvation and spiritual formation in Christ around the world.

The letters the apostle Paul wrote to the fledgling churches of the first century emphasized practice of the spiritual Disciplines as the means by which apprentices of Jesus would grow in the knowledge and character of Christ.

"Train yourself to be godly," Paul wrote, "for physical training is of some value, but godliness has value for all things, holding promise for both the present life and the life to come. . . . Do not conform to the pattern of this world but be transformed by the renewing of your mind. . . . Throw off your old sinful nature and your former way of life . . . let the Spirit renew your thoughts and attitudes. Put on your new nature, created to be like God— truly righteous and holy. . . . We are being transformed into his likeness with ever-increasing glory, which comes from the Lord, who is the Spirit. . . . Therefore, we do not lose heart. Though outwardly we are wasting away, yet inwardly we are being renewed day by day. . . . Each of you is now a new person. You are becoming more and more like your Creator, and you will understand him better. . . . Christ is all that matters, and he lives in each of us."[126]

In the centuries that followed the ministry of the apostle Paul, the Christian faith spread rapidly in all directions, stretching from India and China in the east to Britain in the west, from the Danube in the north to Ethiopia in the south. Christianity was thriving across cultures on three continents.

But major losses followed this early expansion. The legal establishment of Christianity by Rome and Constantinople in the fourth century caused Christianity gradually to seep into European culture; the faith continued to expand but in a diluted form. From the sixteenth to the mid-twentieth centuries, missionaries and immigrants carried the message of the cross to all seven continents. But as the twentieth century dawned, momentum slowed.

In a century marked by a Great Depression, two world wars, the horrors of Auschwitz and Hiroshima, a war in Vietnam, and the advent of global terrorism, expectations swung from optimism to despair and back several times. In 1969, American astronauts traveled to the moon and sent back stunning photographs displaying the beauty of the Earth from space, a beauty that we now saw was being threatened by ecological disaster. The population of Earth had increased sixfold, along with hunger, malnutrition, and poverty. Christianity had spread to about a third of the human population, making its biggest inroads in the southern hemisphere, but was receding in its former homes of Europe and America where an influx of spiritual alternatives was attracting popular attention.

Supported by careful and thorough research, it was now confirmed that in its current and public forms, Christianity was not imparting effectual answers to the vital questions of human existence. At least not to wide ranges of self-identifying Christians and obviously not to non-Christians. This concerning development motivated Richard Foster to take action.

"On a popular level," claims the online encyclopedia *Wikipedia*, "the Spiritual Formation Movement emerged, in part, with the publication of **Richard Foster's** *Celebration of Discipline* in 1978, which introduced a set of spiritual disciplines as historical practices beyond Bible study, prayer, and church attendance that may lead to religious maturity and spiritual growth."[127] Scholar David Pocta confirms this assessment, agreeing that *Celebration of Discipline* was the spark that ignited the movement.[128] It did so, maintains church historian Gerald L. Sittser, by "providing examples of how believers who lived in other times and places understood what it means to seek, know, and experience God."[129]

CELEBRATION OF DISCIPLINE LIGHTS A FIRE

When *Celebration of Discipline* hit bookstore shelves, spiritual practices that had grounded Christians in faith for millennia found a contemporary voice. Like throwing a log onto the embers of a fire, a passion for spiritual formation in Christ leapt into flame, crossing denominational lines and international borders to spark old forms of walking in the Spirit appropriate to our present age.

The sharp uptick of interest in spiritual formation into Christlikeness prompted scores of invitations for Richard Foster to speak, making it apparent that faithful Christians were hungry for what *Celebration of Discipline* promised. Many of them had read the book and were practicing the Disciplines, but still they were struggling.

Howard Baker contends that the problem for most readers was a fundamental disconnect. They practiced the Disciplines hoping to spark a change, yet it eluded them. They worried that they didn't have the "right spiritual stuff" to experience a transformation of heart.[130]

As Richard Foster reflected on what he was seeing and hearing from readers, he drew the same conclusion. People were mistaking the *means* for the *end*. They were centering on the Disciplines themselves as though they were the most important thing. Richard found himself repeatedly stressing, "When we look at the Bible, we don't find a great amount of discussion about the spiritual Disciplines. Oh, it's there, and it's important—but the one thing that is overwhelmingly important in the Bible is hearing and obeying God. The Disciplines are only a way of helping us to do that; they are a way we set ourselves before God. It is *God* who accomplishes the work of transformation in the human heart."[131]

Renováré

Pondering the problem, Richard had an inspiration. What if he were to establish a Christian nonprofit ministry? Richard invited a few friends to test and discern the leading. When they responded positively, in 1988 Richard asked his companions to join him in founding Renováré (the Latin word for *renewal*), whose mission would be "to model, resource, and advocate fullness of life with God experienced, by grace, through the spiritual practices of Jesus and of the historical Church." The team developed a balanced vision of life in Christ and a practical strategy for spiritual formation that they then traveled in pairs to present in different venues all across the United States and around the world.

Dallas Willard, Richard Foster, Bill Vaswig.

The principal medium for the message was the Renovaré regional conferences. Christians from local churches would gather to receive teaching from ministry team members describing God's ongoing presence in a believer's life and the role of the Disciplines as a practical means of grace. The conferences pointed participants beyond individual spiritual formation to present spiritual formation groups as a way to join with others in intentional community.

A participant admitted, "When I first read *Celebration of Discipline*, I was depressed. I knew that I had just read profound truth, but I didn't know what to do with it! Where does one even begin to work on the concepts in the book? Renovaré was

the answer to that question. Foster founded Renovaré to help people like me understand that spiritual formation in Christlikeness takes time (it is not a 'one-and-done' deal) and that it occurs best when embraced with others in community."[132]

At the conclusion of each gathering, attendees were invited to embrace the Renovaré covenant: "In utter dependence upon Jesus Christ as my ever-living Savior,

Teacher, Lord, and Friend, I will seek continual renewal through Spiritual Exercises, Spiritual Gifts, and Acts of Service."

The reach and reputation of Renovaré steadily grew as Richard and the Renovaré ministry team led regional events, retreats, and large-venue national and international conferences. The balanced and practical strategy Renovaré promoted was producing consistent spiritual fruit.

Richard Hovey recounts that the classic spiritual Disciplines he discovered in *Celebration of Discipline* "filled in what had been missing in my spiritual journey." Eager to share his experience with others, Hovey telephoned the Renovaré US office to ask about any ministry plans they might have in Canada. That call started a conversation that led to the founding of Renovaré Canada, with Hovey as its director.[133] In time, other international expressions of the ministry sprang up in Britain and Ireland, Korea and Brazil.

By the turn of the century, the movement sparked by *Celebration of Discipline* was raging across the United States and abroad. Denominational seminaries adopted the language and ethos of spiritual formation, and books and curriculum were being published at an astounding rate. Looking on, Richard Foster could see that some of the resources labeled as "spiritual formation" lacked substance and were "going in all kinds of directions." Solid teaching was needed to establish a clear definition of spiritual formation and a firm biblical foundation for the burgeoning movement.

When Richard discussed his concern with his colleague, Dallas Willard, they agreed that "the spiritual formation field at present lacks intellectual rigor and testable information needed to put the gospel and spiritual life in Christ on the cognitive map for the multitudes of people who are hungry for something real."

Three outcomes resulted from this discussion. First, in order to support the burgeoning demand for a biblical foundation in Christian spiritual formation, a team of scholars gathered to

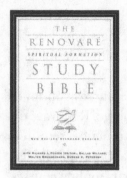

develop the *Renovaré Spiritual Formation Bible* (published in 2005). The Bible captured the reality of living with the Trinitarian community in the ever-present Kingdom of God.

Second, Richard envisioned the establishment of an institute in spiritual formation that would immerse students into Trinitarian life in the Kingdom of God and teach them to actually do what Jesus says is best. The content would include a Christian theology of spirituality, the practice of spiritual Disciplines, and a balanced vision of the "six traditional streams of Christian spirituality" (*Streams of Living Water*, Foster, 1998). The curriculum would blend intellectual rigor with practical experience and individual learning with small group discovery.[134]

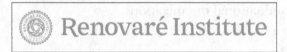

Renovaré Institute

When Richard shared this vision with a group of pastors and scholars, they expressed enthusiastic support for the idea. The Martin Family Foundation provided money to fund the start-up, and, in 2007, Gary W. Moon was hired to prepare a strategic plan and to recommend and design an experimental curriculum. In 2009, the first cohort of the Renovaré Institute: School for Christian Spiritual Formation launched. In 2015, Carolyn Arends succeeded Gary Moon as director of the Renovaré Institute. Under Arends's leadership, the Renovaré Institute continues to flourish.

A third outcome of Richard's discussion with Dallas Willard was a plan to develop a precise definition of what constitutes spiritual formation in Christ. In 2009, a group of spiritual formation scholars, leaders, and authors collaborated to draft a definition that was then reviewed and ratified at the Renovaré

International Conference in San Antonio. Spiritual formation was specifically defined as the "process of being shaped by the Holy Spirit into the likeness of Christ, filled with love for God and the world."[135]

As the demand for spiritual formation resources continued to increase and online resourcing began to emerge, Renovaré developed a strong internet presence providing practical resources for cultivating the with-God life. The Renovaré.org website features articles, a book club, educational webinars, online courses, podcasts, and other resources designed to encourage and promote formation in Christlikeness.

The spiritual formation movement fanned to flame by the publication of *Celebration of Discipline* continues to spread. Today, if you search "Spiritual Formation Programs" you are directed to literally hundreds of degree and certification programs offered by seminaries, universities, colleges, institutes, and denominational organizations.

CHAPTER 10

Compelling Evidence

"Wisdom is proved right by her actions."[136]

Any reader of this book biography might reasonably ask, "But does it work? Does practice of the Disciplines result in real, substantive change?" What follows is the compelling evidence.

Dr. Jeffrey Rediger is part of the faculty at Harvard Medical School. He asserts, "All revolutions are [fueled by personal] stories. They help us see what is possible that wasn't possible before. They paint a picture of a better future, and that is why they come to pass: because when we see it, we can reach for it."[137]

In truth, oftentimes we don't even know what is possible until we see it alive in another person. It was stories of transformation that captured Richard Foster's imagination and set his heart on fire. He wanted for himself what he saw active in the lives of the devotional masters. So, when they described the spiritual Disciplines as the way we may cooperate intentionally with the transformative inner work of the indwelling Holy Spirit, he was all in.

When I met Richard Foster for the first time, the integrity of his faith and life was visibly evident. I wondered, "How did

Richard Foster become Richard Foster? What might I do to experience the same transformative result?"

Others had the same reaction. Roy Searle, one of the founders of the new monastic Northumbrian Community, said that when he invited Richard Foster to present a series of lectures in the UK on the practices described in *Celebration of Discipline*, he noticed that something was different about the bestselling author. Whereas other speakers were often, sadly, one kind of person in front of the group and another behind the scenes, Richard was consistently the same. He lived what he taught. His character bore the quality of someone who spent time in prayer, silence, solitude, worship, and confession. Richard was accessible, kind, generous, and magnanimous which made a distinct impression on Roy and his colleagues.

People who have known Richard Foster for years say the same. Dr. Gayle Beebe, president of Westmont College, said, "If I were to name the one individual who has had the most profound influence on me, it would be Richard Foster. When I first met him at George Fox College in 1977, he was writing *Celebration of Discipline*. I read the manuscript in mimeographed form! I had grown up in Christian circles all my life and yet had never read or experienced such a thorough ordering of how we could understand and make progress in our life with God. It was a thrilling time, full of so many authentic and helpful discoveries that have guided my life ever since."[138]

Beebe, who co-authored a book with Richard, describes Richard as carrying the authority of a contemporary prophetic voice. He cites his mentor's "rare ability to discern the 'themes and threads' of God's activities in the daily affairs of everyday life."[139]

Nancy Thomas came to know Richard when they both were students at George Fox College. When *Celebration of Discipline* was published, she purchased a copy and put the ancient Disciplines into practice. "*Celebration of Discipline* made clear the give-and-take of my growing relationship with Jesus. I 'watered' it by doing what I knew to do—the Disciplines, along with obedience in my daily walk. And Jesus responded by giving grace and growth, as well as fruit. I learned that Discipline and grace are not opposites but close companions."

Nancy Thomas and her husband, Hal, used *Celebration of Discipline* as a primary text when they moved to South America as professors of missiology at the Bolivian Evangelical University. "By that time *Celebration* had been translated into Spanish, and we found not only that the book's content communicated well cross-culturally but that most of our students were already acquainted with the book and familiar with its practices. *Celebration of Discipline* was a resource we relied on."[140]

When Fuller Theological Seminary professor and author Siang Yang Tan met Richard Foster, he knew he had discovered a valued colleague and friend. It was not long before Tan joined the Renovaré ministry team. A native of Singapore, he was introduced early in life to the classic spiritual Disciplines and knew their transformative power. So when Tan read *Celebration of Discipline,* he began at once to promote it as a resource in his pastoral ministry, in his classes in the School of Psychology at Fuller Seminary, and in the books he was writing on spirituality in counseling. "I am deeply grateful to Richard Foster for writing a book that has blessed countless lives—including mine—in helping us to become more like Jesus."[141]

Another prominent psychologist, Gary Collins, praised *Celebration of Discipline* for its deep and powerful contribution both to Christian spirituality and psychological healing. "The book continues to help generations of readers in their walks with Christ."[142]

When all is said and done, says author Valerie Hess, "the real strength of *Celebration of Discipline* is found in its practical application. The only way to transform a society is to have transformed people within it. *Celebration of Discipline* gives readers the practical steps needed to make this happen."[143]

National political consultant Jon Kohan feels the same. "I don't know where I would be today had I not picked up and read the book. *Celebration* is on my desk at Jamestown Associates and is rarely more than an arm's reach away. I have purchased a copy for others and talk about it constantly. Practicing the Disciplines is what has drawn me close to God and laid out the path I am following."[144]

Robert Chestnut credits *Celebration of Discipline* for saving his life. "For some time, I had been in a spiritual desert—alone and seemingly forgotten by God. Then one day Jesus led my wife, Audrey, to stumble across a copy of *Celebration of Discipline* in a thrift store. She and I read it together and spent the next year rediscovering our connection with Jesus. I no longer feel isolated; Jesus is with me, and I am with him. Audrey and I practice the Disciplines every day as a way to connect intentionally with Jesus. *Celebration of Discipline* is a godsend."[145]

In stories like these, readers convey the sense that Jesus put the book into their hands at the very moment they needed it the most. Former medical missionary and Renovaré ministry team member Marti Ensign could not agree more. A follower of Christ since childhood, reading *Celebration of Discipline* showed Ensign that there was a depth to being a Christ follower that she knew nothing about or even thought possible. "Practicing the Disciplines as a way to draw close to Jesus changed me forever, and I am still being changed."[146]

Carolyn Arends was a popular Canadian Christian recording artist traveling with her band when the bass player, Dave, lent her his copy of *Celebration of Discipline*. On a long bus trip, Arends began to read. "Willpower will never succeed in dealing with the deeply ingrained habits of sin. The demand is for an *inside* job, and only God can work from the inside. But hear the good news, God has given us the Disciplines of the spiritual life as a means of receiving his grace. The Disciplines allow us to place ourselves before God so he can transform us."

Arends had never heard this before. Scanning the table of contents, she saw that some of the Disciplines were new to her while others were "old friends." But *Celebration of*

Discipline successfully reframed the way she thought about them. Accustomed to viewing the Disciplines as chores, she now understood them to be ways we may "progressively and systematically rearrange the habits of our life" in order to know God more intimately, more personally. Eager to grow deep in God, Arends purchased her own copy of *Celebration of Discipline* and dug in.[147]

Reverend Doctor Derek Oppenshaw is a Methodist minister serving in South Africa. Like Arends, he admits to having viewed the Disciplines as a "dull drudgery with more than a hint of legalism." Then one day he lifted *Celebration of Discipline* (1978) off a dusty bookshelf. As he curiously ran his finger down the table of contents, "A chapter heading drew my attention—a simple heading which was to ignite a paradigm shift: 'The Spiritual Disciplines: Door to Liberation!'"

Liberation!? This was not a word Oppenshaw associated with discipline of any sort. His curiosity piqued, he began to read. "Foster presented the Disciplines as a way we may place ourselves in a position where God's Spirit can work with us the best and most directly."[148] More than four decades after its original publication, Oppenshaw still recommends *Celebration of Discipline* to his colleagues and friends as a vital means of God's transforming grace—the door to liberation!

Andrew Arndt was given a copy of *Celebration*, when he was seventeen years of age, from his mother, whose pastor had recommended it to her. "Reading *Celebration of Discipline* lit my world on fire! It wasn't just what the book said, or even how it was communicated, it was the way that the book introduced me to my spiritual ancestors—mothers and fathers, aunties and uncles, brothers and sisters in the faith . . . a cloud of witnesses whose lives still spoke and whose wells of wisdom I could drink from whenever I wished. *Celebration* introduced me to spiritual formation in Christ and set a whole new course for my life work as a pastor."[149]

Celebration of Discipline initiated a journey for Arndt that later led to reading Foster's *Streams of Living Water*. Eager to form a church around the vision embodied both in *Celebration* and *Streams*, Arndt planted Bloom Church in Denver, Colorado—a neo-monastic, charismatic, liturgical, justice-oriented network of house churches. "As an evangelical minister, I was already concerned that a one-dimensional theology of 'just make a decision for Jesus' wasn't enough to form fully devoted followers of Jesus." Members of Arndt's church covenanted to practice a congregational "Rule of Life" incorporating the spiritual Disciplines, endeavoring in all they did to live incarnationally. "I must tell you," Arndt smiles, "the Disciplines really *work!*"

Korean Pastor Joshua Choonmin Kang was studying in the United States when a ministerial colleague gave him a copy of *Celebration of Discipline,* describing it as the best resource he knew on spiritual formation. Kang was uncertain, as he found the practice of spiritual Disciplines to be very hard. Reading the book changed his mind. "I now saw that spiritual Disciplines are a means of divine grace for our inner transformation; they help us become like Jesus!"

This realization gave Kang a vision. "I knew that *Celebration of Discipline* could help the Korean church to pursue the spirituality of depth that was lacking. By God's grace, the church had grown very rapidly. But while the church grew rapidly, regretfully, it lacked depth. Pastors were serving the church energetically, but they weren't presenting spiritual formation in Christlikeness. I saw that *Celebration of Discipline* could help our pastors promote a deeper life, not a superficial one."

When Kang introduced *Celebration of Discipline* to his pastoral colleagues, his enthusiastic support convinced them to read it. Before long, churches across South Korea were asking Richard Foster to come teach the Disciplines to overflowing crowds. Several of these invitations he accepted.

Considering all that has transpired in South Korea through the influence of Richard's seminal book, Pastor Kang says, "The spiritual Disciplines taught in *Celebration of Discipline* go beyond human effort. They are infused with the grace of God through the Holy Spirit to lead disciples of Christ into sanctification and glorification. Nothing is more beautiful and happy than being like Jesus." [150]

EMPIRICAL EVIDENCE

Personal stories like these confirm the transformative influence that *Celebration of Discipline* has had. The subjective evidence abounds. In recent years these claims have received substantial empirical support in the findings of neuroscience. Studies of brain function reveal that the practice of intentional, disciplined behaviors possesses the powerful ability to literally reconfigure the brain's neurological networks.

"Neuroplasticity," explains J. P. Moreland, "refers to the brain's ability to form new brain grooves—new patterns of synaptic connections—and undergo a change of structure. The brain is not stuck in a static, unchanging structure. In fact, through repeated habit-forming practices of different ways of thinking, feeling, and behaving, one can reshape one's brain in a healthy direction. But this reshaping requires three things: *practice, practice, practice*! Practice doesn't make perfect; it makes permanent."[151]

Neuroscientist Curt Thompson verifies,

We describe the brain as having a great deal of plasticity. This refers to its capacity, at a cellular connection level, to make new synapses and to prune away those synapses that don't get much firing action. . . . This neuroplasticity can be enhanced and facilitated by our intentional behavior. . . . A vast array of our mental and physical actions follow what we attend to. . . . When you select the target of your focus, the dorsolateral prefrontal cortex begins to act like a spotlight, making synaptic connections with the other layers of

119

neuronal tissue that correspond to the various aspects of what you are concentrating on. It shines a light on the multitude of different elements of the brain that are coming together to help form what you are focusing on. . . . The way we attend to elements of our experience *wires* our brains in certain patterns.

"We now understand," echoes Australian psychologist Katherine Thompson, "that the brain is a dynamic organ that can heal and alter its functioning by creating new connections between cells where the practicing of new skills has produced alternative neural pathways. The more we *practice* these techniques, the stronger the neural pathways for these skills are forged in our brain. Essentially, we are changing our thoughts, feelings and behaviours through repetition."[152]

Long before neuroscientists possessed the technical ability to track the physiological effects of habitual Discipline, Christians understood their transformative value. "Do not conform any longer to the pattern of this world but be transformed by the renewing of your mind. Then you will be able to test and approve what God's will is—his good, pleasing, and perfect will."[153] Brain science gives us just another way to understand what transpires when we intentionally cooperate with the Holy Spirit in our spiritual formation.

A SURPRISING EXCHANGE

Just as remarkable—and surprising—is the growing body of evidence for the "heart to heart communication" that occurs when people gather in close proximity.

Every human being has what neuroscientists describe as an "extended brain," referring to the brain's connections, via cranial and peripheral nerves, to other organs, most notably the viscera (the heart, lungs, and digestive tract). According to Childre and Rozman, "The heart's electromagnetic field has forty to sixty times more amplitude than that of the brain," allowing it to be measured at a distance of ten feet from the heart muscle.[154] This is one reason why a person's emotional state can be picked up and internalized by another person within a range of ten feet or more. "The field changes with different internal emotions," explains J. P. Moreland, "and as the field changes, it communicates different 'messages,' triggering positive or negative thoughts."[155] Our emotional state, as a result, reflects not only our own inner neural and experiential activity, but that from our interactions with the neural and experiential activity of other's minds.[156]

For two decades, neuroscientist and psychiatrist Jeffrey Rediger has been researching this fascinating communal phenomenon. On the recommendation of a patient, he visited a spiritual healing center in Brazil where people with serious illness had gathered for guided meditation. "The sense of community was strong, and many people experienced genuine, deep connections in a few short days that seemed to run deeper and wider than anything they had at home. There was a current of energy that ran from person to person, so electric that even I could feel it."[157] No matter whether we are aware of it, Rediger asserts, we are deeply influenced by the contingent emotional experience of the people around us.

Jesuit Herbert Alfonso is familiar with the phenomenon Rediger describes. Alfonso goes so far as to suggest that "a person becomes a person only within community; and a community is a true community only if it is made up of responsible persons where the members are making the communal goal of spiritual formation responsibly their own."[158] Quaker Robert Barclay uses the imagery of candles to describe the shared effect. "As many candles lighted and put in one place do greatly augment the light, and makes it more to shine forth; so, when many are gathered together into the same Life, there is more of the glory of God, and his power appears to the refreshment of each individual present."[159]

"This is a power known only by experience," explains Caroline Stephen, "and mysterious even when familiar. The presence of fellow-worshipers in some gently penetrating manner reveals to the spirit something of the nearness of the Divine Presence."[160]

Years of observing the deep interpersonal communication that transpires between individuals and the potential of its restorative effect compels psychiatrist and neuroscientist Bruce Perry to confirm Herbert Alfonso's belief that "most healing happens in the context of community."

It is no surprise in the context of this unfolding research that the whole of Scripture points toward the idea that God is not first and foremost focused on our individual salvation. As Curt Thompson contends, "God's desire is to redeem the entire world, and we as a body of people, inextricably connected to one another, are being saved in the process and for that very purpose."[161]

The evidence is compelling. The robust vitality of *Celebration of Discipline* is not limited to personal transformation. It is best understood in its broad presentation of a time-tested, biblically based, spiritually reliable, empirically commended means to cooperate with the Holy Spirit in the transformation of entire communities of people with a view to changing the world.

CHAPTER 11

The Transcendent Character of
Celebration of Discipline

What unique qualities in *Celebration of Discipline* give it a transcendent character? Why has it not faded in the way that other books on spiritual practices published in the 1980s and 1990s have done? What accounts for the genius and ongoing appeal of this groundbreaking book? In recent years, many commentators have endeavored to provide an account. What follows is a distillation of the insights that represent a consensus of opinion.

A COMPELLING VISION

British Anglican Austin Farrer commented that while reading *Celebration of Discipline*, "We may think we are listening to an argument; in fact, we are presented with a vision; and it is the vision that carries conviction."[162] It is practical and attainable without being legalistic or heroic (requiring an aesthetic life lived apart).

In the foreword to the special fortieth anniversary edition, Richard Foster explains, "If you are anything like me, you genuinely long for abilities that are beyond yourself in order to face the demands of everyday life patiently and wisely. You—I—*we*—would love to have the inner resources to replace deep, destructive habits of thought with even deeper, life-giving habits of mind and heart and spirit. . . . Throughout the ages, Christians of all races and ethnicities from all geographical locations and economic backgrounds have witnessed that the classical Disciplines of the spiritual life can produce deep within us exactly this kind of life. The spiritual Disciplines are the *means* of God's grace for bringing about genuine personality formation characterized through and through by love and joy and peace and patience and kindness and goodness and faithfulness and gentleness and self-control (Galatians 5:22–23). . . . If we truly desire to be like Jesus, then we will want to take up the overall way of life Jesus himself lived when he was among us in the flesh. We learn from the Gospels of Matthew, Mark, Luke, and John that Jesus undertook spiritual Disciplines as a fixed pattern of his life. So should we. This is a life for ordinary people, people just like you and me."[163]

Had Richard Foster simply presented his own personal views, *Celebration of Discipline* might well have had little lasting impact. This is not to minimize his role as author; his character, integrity, and humility shine through. But Richard did not simply present arguments; rather, he wrote like a friendly companion on a journey, highlighting the beliefs and practices that have been common to virtually all Christians at all times. *Celebration of Discipline* presents a compelling vision for a life with God as something that can be seen, experienced, and enjoyed as the most beautiful and joyful of all realities.[164]

PRACTICES FOR KINGDOM LIVING HERE AND NOW

Dallas Willard identified the book's practical approach to living life in the Kingdom of God as being its most significant contribution. "History has brought us to the point where the Christian message is thought to be *essentially* concerned *only* with how to deal with sin and its effects," writes Willard. "Life, our actual existence, is not included in what is now presented as the heart of the Christian message, or it is included only marginally. This is where we find ourselves today. The current gospel has become 'a gospel of sin management.' Widespread acceptance of this interpretation of salvation has created a situation in which those who profess Christian commitment consistently show little or no behavioral and psychological difference from those who do not. Salvation has been effectively separated from everyday life leaving us with the belief that our becoming more like Christ is a distant hope reserved for our eternity in heaven."[165]

Celebration of Discipline confronted this detachment of faith from life by directing full attention to the person of Jesus Christ who demonstrates in word and in deed the reality of an eternal life lived *now* under God's rule. Jesus told his disciples, "Follow me!" *Celebration of Discipline* teaches that when we do what we see Jesus doing, making his spiritual practices our own, we begin living *today* as we will for all eternity in God's heaven.

BOTH ACCESSIBLE AND CHALLENGING

In researching this biography, recent converts conveyed their gratitude for the help *Celebration of Discipline* had given their developing relationship with God. While many church programs stopped at conversion, *Celebration of Discipline* gave these readers practical, accessible ways that they could cooperate with the Holy Spirit in their transformation into Christlikeness. Seasoned followers of "The Way" reported being helped and challenged by its teaching, while novice Christians described the book as a godsend.

As mentioned earlier, Roy Searle is one of the founders of the new monastic Northumbrian Community. A mature follower of Christ who came from an unchurched background, Roy rereads *Celebration of Discipline* every year during the season of

Lent. As he sits with and practices each of the twelve individual Disciplines, he continues to be enlightened and encouraged by the practices, often encountering Christ in fresh, new ways.

COMMUNITY-BASED WHILE
ALLOWING INDIVIDUAL EXPRESSION

The spiritual practices *Celebration of Discipline* teaches begin with the individual. The inner Disciplines of meditation, prayer, fasting, and study seat the believer in an interactive relationship with the Trinity, facilitating the individual's formation into Christlikeness. While the nature of this communion is deeply intimate and personal, it shares formational characteristics with the experience of others on the same journey.

The outward Disciplines of simplicity, solitude, submission, and service give shape to the way that individuals express their relationship with God in the circumstances of everyday life. The means of expression is as unique to individual believers as are our fingerprints. But if we stop there, if we limit our formation in Christ to our personal experience, we miss out on the best part of what God makes available.

In a culture known for its rugged individualism, *Celebration of Discipline* presents a picture of what can happen when individuals immersed in the inner and outer Disciplines gather in community. A blossoming occurs. Jesus promises, "Where two or three are gathered together in my name, I will be there in their midst" (Matthew 18:20). The corporate Disciplines of confession, worship, guidance, and celebration propel believers into the presence of the triune God in a way that is far greater than the sum of the individual parts. We hear differently. We see differently. In community, we experience God differently. And we are transformed. It is beautiful. It is miraculous. We don't want to miss out.

Timeless Truths

Richard Foster avoided the trap of "chronological snobbery." A student of Christian history, Richard understood the tendency to regard history as an "evolutionary progression from earlier, more primitive times of relative ignorance toward the triumph of modern scientifically based illumination."[166] But Richard also understood that in times of significant cultural transition, people need perspective from the past in order to recognize that much of which seems certain to the ill-informed is merely temporary fashion. Readers in recent times have found the timeless truths preserved in *Celebration of Discipline* to be as helpful and relevant as they were in times long past, contributing to the ongoing influence of this contemporary classic.

Avoids Being Culturally Bound

Richard Foster avoided tying *Celebration of Discipline* to the tumultuous political or social issues of his day. He determined, instead, to write a book that was tethered to perennial truths and would, as a result, be as relevant in one hundred years' time as it was the first day it appeared on book stands. Richard's avoidance of culturally bound issues and references contributes to the lasting vitality of this book.

Bridging Ecclesiastical Barriers

In responding to *Celebration of Discipline*'s promise of a deeper life with God through practice of the classic spiritual Disciplines, Roman Catholics, Eastern Orthodox, Anglicans, Presbyterians, Methodists, Baptists, Lutherans, Adventists, and loyalists representing a variety of other denominations have recognized and embraced their commonalities with fellow Christians. *Celebration of Discipline* has provided a practical ecumenism among believers sharing a core of perennial Christian commitments.

Roman Catholic Brandon Vogt writes, "As a young man, *Celebration of Discipline* introduced me to several new spiritual masters—Augustine, Teresa of Avila, Julian of Norwich, and Brother Lawrence. The book affirmed that I didn't have to grope down the path of faith, for these masters up and down the Christian centuries had already paved the way. I merely had to follow their steps, habitually and intentionally. *Celebration of Discipline* contains a wealth of riches for many Christian traditions. It leads Christians forward by taking them backward into the great Christian tradition. This explains why *Celebration of Discipline*, a book containing ancient wisdom, is paradoxically a modern classic. I'm convinced it will remain so for many years to come."[167]

CONCLUDING OBSERVATION

The fact that *Celebration of Discipline* has been in continuous publication since 1978 with sales, in English alone, that number well over two million hardback copies attests to the life-changing, perspective-altering influence this book has had. This chapter highlights seven qualities that account for the book's transcendent character, but the list is far from exhaustive. It is expected that with time, *Celebration's* distinctive influence will continue to expand, extending well beyond the movement it sparked. We move now to imagine what this influence will be and where it leads.

Chapter 12

Peering Through a Glass Darkly: Where Do We Go From Here?

As we conclude our review of the life and career of this remarkable book, we turn our gaze toward the future to ask, *Where do we go from here?* I (Mimi Dixon) explored this question in a conversation with Richard Foster and his son, Nathan (Nate) Foster.

Mimi: When we consider the fullest expression of the movement *Celebration of Discipline* started, we observe that it has had both an individual and a corporate expression. If individuals are willing to place themselves before the Lord to be transformed, this receptive posture will result in the transformation of communities, which, in turn, will have a transformative effect on individuals. It is a beautiful symbiotic relationship.

Richard: It is. I recently saw this in practice. I had gone to see my brother because he felt he might not have much longer to live. When the little church community that he is a part of heard that he was doing poorly, they gathered to be with him; they invited me to be a part of their group. They listened carefully and helped my brother plot a path forward. It was a very special time for him. And for me too. The continuing effects have been especially significant; he's so much better! Oh, and his friends are committed to staying with him in very practical ways in the weeks and months to come.

Mimi: I am so glad to hear that your brother is doing better, and his friends are *really* helping him! Your story reminds me of something the late Desmond Tutu said, "There comes a point where we need to stop just pulling people out of the river. We need to go upstream and find out why they're falling in."

Richard: Tutu is exactly right. Of course, we must start with individuals, right where they are, and we teach them how to swim so they can hopefully get out of the river. This may include some action to stabilize the person, but we begin *there,* right where they are. Then as Tutu said we go upriver to discover the cause of the trouble. This is what my brother's friends are doing for him. They are staying close and keeping him from "falling in." Most of the time, this involves spiritual Disciplines in one form or another.

I have been significantly helped by others in community. In the early days, you know, I was trying to be heroically spiritual like John Wesley or Teresa of Avila. I learned that John Wesley rose at 4 a.m. to pray, so I would rise at 4 a.m. to pray. But I kept falling asleep. So, I would stand up against a wall . . . do you know you can fall asleep standing against a wall? [Laughter]. The point is I could never measure up. I always failed. But then some dear people came around me and helped. For some, it might be a small group of friends who meet weekly for prayer and fellowship. For others, it might be just one other person. We always start where we are.

Nate: I hear several things in this, but what stands out is the importance of community in spiritual formation. This is not something that we do on our own.

Richard: Yes [enthusiastically]! Your work in Renovaré with the Fellowship of the Burning Heart is a good example.

Nate: We actually started that initiative with people like your brother in mind. People were coming to us saying, "I need God, and I need community." They came humbly, with openness and a deep desire to grow spiritually. We listened to their request and developed the Fellowship of the Burning Heart. The parameters of the gatherings keep it safe for honest sharing and mutual support to take place. I've noticed that when a group of people hungry for God gather in community, Jesus *always* shows up.

Mimi: This has been my experience as well. For over twenty years I have been part of a small fellowship of pastors. We called ourselves "The Company of the Failed" [Laughter]. We called ourselves that because our churches were small. But what really drew us together was our shared hunger for the Lord and awareness that we needed each other to grow deeper in our life with God.

Nate: Nice! So, how did it work? What did you do?

Mimi: We listened each other into an awareness of what none of us could see on our own. We helped one another recognize and name our experiences of God.

Nate: So, spiritual formation occurred naturally as you listened to one another?

Mimi: Yes, that has been our experience.

Nate: Hey, Dad, some people think you can package this into a program.

Richard: Transformation cannot be programmed; it is the sole work of the Holy Spirit. *But* Jesus does promise to be present when two or more gather in his name. Which is what I noticed as I listened to the two of you describe your experience.

This is important: you identified the characteristics of a transformational community. I heard you say that it is relational, it is adaptive, and it is rooted in listening—to God and to the person talking. I would add a fourth characteristic: *longevity*—it takes time for a culture like this to develop.

. In my early years as a pastor, I was preaching through the Old Testament book of Exodus. I had just described the way that Moses tried to do the work of God in the power of the flesh and that it took him forty years to learn to do the work of God in the power of the Spirit. Hopefully, I concluded, it will not take *us* forty years to learn that like it did Moses.

As was acceptable in our congregational context, someone spoke up. It was Dallas Willard. He said, "I doubt it" [Laughter].

We discovered that spiritual formation into Christlikeness takes time to develop. You can't cut corners by means of clever programming or crafting ten steps to holiness. Formation takes time. We must learn to come into rhythm with the Holy Spirit, to align ourselves with the cosmic patience of God. So, give it time to develop. God can be trusted to take it from there.

Mimi: This is good counsel, Richard. *Celebration of Discipline* presents the spiritual practices as a way we may cooperate with the Holy Spirit in our transformation into Christlikeness. We cannot "make" anything happen, but we can give our people a vision and a taste, and—space and time.

When I first introduced my congregation *Celebration*, people were curious, but the overall response was neutral. Some people were very eager to learn more. Others said, "I don't want this." The largest group was in the middle. One aspect of longevity is that transformation takes a while—in our case, years. What eventually turned the tide was the evidence of changed lives. This outcome was clearly a gift of God's grace, not the result of anything we programmed to make happen.

Nate: I would agree that spiritual formation cannot be programmed. People have to *choose*. One of the prerequisites for the Fellowship of the Burning Heart is that people must apply to join. They are interviewed to confirm that they understand the commitment involved. They promise to give the group priority in their monthly schedule. This is what makes the group work. When the six strangers then meet and begin telling their stories, something beautiful happens. They connect. They bond. Now the commitment is personal. They say, "This is a priority! I can let other things slide but not my Burning Heart group."

Richard: I see in this an entirely fresh expression of what the church may become. For the most part, this isn't tied to buildings, and it isn't tied to cash. Over time, even the liturgical expressions we are accustomed to may likely change and new liturgies emerge. Transformational communities are personal, relational, and adaptive. And they are alive with the Holy Spirit! People are continually growing in their hunger for God, which is deeply contagious.

Mimi: This is exciting to contemplate! Nathan, I'm curious, is there a shared commitment in the Burning Heart groups to practice the spiritual Disciplines?

Nate: Yes. Participants commit to individual practices, and what they share in the group comes out of what they have experienced in their time with God. But here is the odd thing. People often do not even know what they are bringing until something happens in the group that causes it to emerge, and they become aware of it. I've seen this over and over again. Like you said before, Mimi, in sharing with others what they have experienced with God, people actually "see" more. That is why longevity is so essential to these little pockets of community.

Richard: Speaking of longevity, recently, I've been thinking about another important aspect of community—one that isn't limited by space or time. The "Blessed Community," as Thomas Kelly puts it, where even the incident of death puts no boundary on community life. Kelly says that when we read the Scriptures we discover "friends for the soul"— friends like Hosea, Amos, and Isaiah who teach us about a life lived in God's presence. These soul friends show us how to experience God's vivid guidance in our own lives, for we feed on the same life as they did and are caught up in the same holy flame that was burning in their hearts.

Kelly describes "the volcanic upheaving, shaggy power of the prophets." Isn't that wonderful! And then, when he is describing Jesus in the Gospels, Kelly talks about the "blinding, wooing, winning, overcoming love of Jesus of Nazareth." Isn't that simply stunning! All of the biblical people are part of the Blessed Community and are available to us as "friends for the soul."

Mimi: I love this vision of unbroken fellowship! I recognize in Kelly's words an echo of the same vision that shaped and formed *Celebration of Discipline*. The book presents a life with God that is available to anyone, making it clear that we don't have to be a Mother Teresa or a Saint Francis or a Desmond Tutu to experience life with God. In the Blessed Community, we learn from and journey with soul friends from the biblical past, in our current lives, and even with loved ones who have passed into God's heaven. We journey together into a deeper life with God.

Richard: Yes, there are these two great rhythms in the Christian life. There is the uniquely individual life of each one of us—"that solitary individual," as Kierkegaard put it. Remember the old spiritual, "Jesus Walked this Lonesome Valley," where the song goes on to remind us, "I must walk this lonesome valley, I have to walk it by myself; O' nobody else can walk it for me, I have to walk it by myself."

And then again, God has created each of us for connection, for life together. This puts relationship right at the center of life. To be effective, formation requires a relational connection.

Nate: When you think about the influence of *Celebration of Discipline*, where do you see that combination of individual and corporate symbiosis? What is the ripple effect?

Richard: I really like your term, "ripple effect." Isn't it lovely to watch ripples of new life pop up in the most unusual places? We marvel at it. We never want the Disciplines to be turned into a technique; we simply allow the "ripples" to flow all over the place. And they will be different in different places.

For example, let's say that somebody operates a retreat center serving different groups that come in. The groups will stay together for only a short time, and yet they are able to develop wonderful relationships and connections. And there are long-term small groups like we've described already. All of these expressions are "ripples."

Nate: I love your purity of thought about this. As formation has entered the academic and ecclesiastical contexts, however, there is this push to come up with graphs and charts and programs. What would you say to people who are caught up in this as a way to manage spiritual progress?

Richard: Ichabod! [Laughter]

We have to get it clear in our heads that we do not *manage* our spiritual progress—or anyone else's. No, NO! Managing is simply not our business. Of course, there are things for us to do. Grace is opposed to works but not effort. We undertake tasks as the Lord leads us, but let's leave the "managing" to God where it belongs. One of the great dangers for the spiritual formation movement is to degenerate into techniques and procedures. Formation is about *life*, not technique. It goes wrong when our practice of the Disciplines is turned into a system, a legalism, *the* way to blessedness.

Nate: So, if people were to use *Celebration of Discipline* as you envision, what would it look like?

Richard: First of all, we remind ourselves that what we are seeking is life with Jesus in the Kingdom of God. Life that is *life* indeed. Second, we undertake Disciplines appropriate to our needs, which will enable us to train in the spiritual life. Third, remember that this is done in the context of a loving, nurturing community.

So, I would tell people to start with *Celebration* right where they are. No need to be heroic about this. Just begin where you are. And find some soul friends to journey with you. Learn their story. Develop the *ecclesiola* in the *ecclesia,* the "little church within the church," as John Wesley put it. We are finding many little ways to gather around Christ, our present Teacher.

Always insist that the focus be your relationship with God, the with-God life that we're after, and not on how to master one practice or another. One practice might help this individual; another practice is what will help that individual. We learn the heart of the person, and spiritual Disciplines appropriate for the individual will flow out of this life together.

We don't try to nail any of this down too tight. In my opinion, it is futile to try to measure this or that. We can know that a person is growing spiritually when they are more loving. That's how we know. But it's not because we've made up a chart with twelve practices to measure how we are doing [Laughter]. We must never try to button formation down too tightly. These things are fluid and change over time as we follow divine grace. Remember the words of Jean-Pierre de Caussade, "The soul, light as a feather, fluid as water, innocent as a child, responds to every movement of grace like a floating balloon."

Mimi: This is so helpful because we can take our progress very seriously—especially as leaders. When I imagined the ideal transformative community, I pictured an outpost of heaven on earth—very high and lifted up. I shared this image with a pastor friend who smiled at the notion and suggested that if a community is a healing community, it might look and function a lot more like a hospital emergency room. There will be blood on the floor. People will be doing triage and offering critical care. And no one will feel the need to project a holy hologram, saying, "I've got it all together. I'm good." They will instead be free to be where they are in their journey toward God.

Richard: Your story reminds me of a Christian psychologist I worked with years ago. He told me about a group counseling meeting he facilitated with some actors in Hollywood. When the group first gathered, they were all being really nice and polite. And then one of them arrived late, flopped into a chair, and declared flatly, "I don't know about the rest of you, but I have had a hell of a day!" Her honest declaration opened up the whole group experience.

Nate: So a question for pastors to ask one another might be: How is our congregation functioning as an ER?

Mimi: You may be right, Nate. People come to an ER knowing that they need help. They are not pretending. And the community has to be safe if people are going to have the courage to be vulnerable. There cannot be a spirit of judgment or condemnation.

Nate: In my experience, the leader sets the tone. If the leader is projecting a "holy hologram," the congregation will pick that up and reflect it. If the leader is genuinely authentic, the congregation will pick that up. The leader sets the tone for the community.

So, Dad, how does all this tie back to *Celebration of Discipline*? Where do you see the connection?

Richard: Recognizing that a transformational community functions as a spiritual ER allows us to do what is needed in the moment.

I know that some people have been put off by the word "discipline" in the title of the book. But what about this word? Discipline is a good word describing the ability to do what needs to be done when it needs to be done—to be response-*able*. That's what discipline is. It is discipline that produces liberty. And that is worth celebrating!

For example, a great pianist is able to play with joy and finesse because of her discipline. That is true in every aspect of life, and it's also true in the spiritual life. That is why discipline is a great liberation. When most people hear the word "discipline," they are thinking not of discipline but of rigidity. This is a misunderstanding. Discipline, remember, produces the ability to do what we need to do *when* we need to do it—like a musician or a skilled athlete. This is why the early Christians spoke of themselves as the *athlete Dei*, "the athletes of God." Discipline is the way God trains us into Christlikeness.

Nate: You are not approaching the Disciplines as something we do to make God like us. You are thinking of discipline as a way that we respond to God's love, a way of falling deeper in love. So how we approach the Disciplines matters!

Richard: And the end result matters—what we're after is a with-God kind of life.

Nate: So, the Disciplines are not twelve more reasons to beat myself up? [Laughter]

Richard: [Emphatically] *Exactly!* I remember in the early days that people would sometimes come, and they were so intense and worried about their growth or lack of growth in Christlikeness. And I'd say, "Just relax a bit and experience life. Learn to sit with Jesus and enjoy a baseball game! Or take a walk. Or play with your kids. Go on a bike ride. Learn to live your whole life in the company of Jesus."

Mimi: That is so helpful! When Teresa of Avila had a sister under her care who was anxious about getting the Disciplines just right in order to get something going with God, Teresa would tell her to lay off the Disciplines for a little while, get out of her room, and do something beautiful for someone else.

Nate: That, in and of itself, *is* a spiritual Discipline.

Mimi: It is! Which brings to mind a question several people asked when I was conducting research for this biography. It concerns the three divisions in *Celebration of Discipline*—the inner, outer, and corporate practices. Richard, why did you shape the book in this fashion? How did you determine which Discipline to include where?

Richard: [Laughing] Oh, my! Well, it is far from a perfect way of describing things, but I was trying to move across the entire range of human experience. First, that we would give careful attention to the inner recesses of the human heart. But the inward work cannot stand alone—we need to move outward toward hurting, broken humanity. So, the second movement is the movement outward. Finally, we do not experience the inner and outward movements in isolation. No, no. The third movement is corporate so that we are living out our lives in relationship with a grace-filled, loving community.

I often use the image of ocean waves to describe the different categories of the Disciplines. They're separate, yet they overlap each other; they all work together. There are inward-focused practices because it's a hidden life; there are aspects of what goes on here that I don't even know about. The transformation of the heart is hidden. I can't transform my heart. And so, I wait upon God. And then there are outward Disciplines, which move us into service toward others, and finally corporate practices that we engage in as a community.

Nate: You are saying that what we need is a whole vision of what it means to be human, that this was your reasoning behind the inward / outward / corporate divisions, that the whole human self is involved in spiritual transformation. The Disciplines draw every part of us into formation and connect us with other people.

Richard: Exactly.

Nate: So, if we were to follow the ripple effect of *Celebration of Discipline*, where do you think this movement is headed?

Richard: Well, first of all, we are not in control of what happens, nor should we try to control what happens—this is the surest way to make a mess of things. Having said that, the future potentially takes us in a thousand different directions depending on the individual. I have always loved the image of the Celtic pilgrims who would get into a coracle, a tiny boat with no rudder, and trust God to blow them wherever God wanted them to go.

Nate: Are you saying we shouldn't do anything? Do you have any idea how ridiculous that sounds? [Laughter]. Just sit in a boat and wait for the wind to blow us along? [More laughter].

Richard: Remember that formation in Christ is not a program. It is not a methodology. It is a *life*. There can be planning, of course, and there can be strategy. But these things are not central to what we are seeking. Jesus told us to seek first the Kingdom of God and the righteousness (that is, right living) that is tied to this Kingdom, and all these things would be added to us. Life in the Kingdom of God is our first priority.

Nate: So, we might think of the Disciplines as guardrails that keep us centered on God? What would you say then to people who think that to please God they must practice all twelve Disciplines all the time?

Richard: [Emphatically] *No way!* Attempting to practice all twelve all the time is a sure way to drive yourself to despair.

Mimi: This really takes the pressure off. I'm thinking about an illustration you used earlier. When a musician is memorizing a difficult concerto, she will repeat a particular phrase over and over, not just to memorize the notes but as a means to embody the music and give it full expression. In similar fashion, in certain seasons or passages of life, we may be led to practice some of the Disciplines more intentionally.

Richard: That sounds right to me. Trying to do all the Disciplines all the time implies a rigidity. That, by its very nature, is soul-crushing. We don't want rigidity. We want *life*—a deeper, fuller life with God. We practice what is needed when it is needed.

Nate: This is good news for everyone and, in particular, for people who have experienced significant trauma. For these folks, practice of the Disciplines can present a real challenge. Silence, for example, can be particularly difficult and damaging when the internal voices turn negative. I suspect that the gift of a healing church community is to know when to gently nudge someone to get professional help and to know how best to support them in the healing process.

Richard: This underscores the importance of really getting to know a person so that we are aware when a particular Discipline can be a danger. We don't press.

Nate: This is also why, when people ask which Disciplines they should practice, I simply say they should ask God. What

I mean is, don't feel pressured to practice the Disciplines in some prescribed manner. Find a way to be with God in your particular context. We just point people to God.

Richard: Yes. We point people to God. This is one of the things I really appreciate in George Fox as a leader; he would always seek to take people's attention off of himself and direct them to Jesus, their present Teacher.

Nate: That is good—hey, I want to go back to something we talked about a little earlier. We suggested that a formational congregation might look a little like an ER. I want to add to that; there is a point where we begin to get better.

Mimi: That is really important, Nate; we do get better. This is a wonderful gift from God. People get better. A healthy church community is like a group of people climbing a steep, snowy mountain. Tethered together for safety, we rotate positions; we take turns leading. In a healthy community, no one has to pretend. We're not always at our best; it isn't always our gold star day; some days we need help. We give help, and we receive help. We "get well" together.

Richard: That is why the spiritual formation groups from Renovaré's earlier days and the current Fellowship of the Burning Heart work so well. We journey together toward a deepening life with God that finds expression in the way that we live in the world. William Penn wrote, "True religion does not draw [us] out of the world but enables [us] to live better in it and excites [our] endeavors to mend it."[168]

Nate: Our conversation today gives me hope for where the movement that *Celebration of Discipline* sparked is headed. I'm hopeful for a number of reasons. I'm hopeful because denominations are now engaging in friendly collaboration. And people are discovering the value of small communities where it is easier to find your soul friends. I think we'll continue to see that. Most of all, we see in history that, during difficult periods, the Holy Spirit ignited entire communities of people with a passionate hunger for God. We are seeing evidence of this happening in our own time as people, hungry for a life with God and filled with love for their neighbors, take hold of the Kingdom of God and bring it to life. It is your "I See a People," Dad.[169] It gives me hope.

Richard: Changed individuals change families that, in turn, transform churches and radiate goodness out into the world.

Nate: The ripple effect. It's the Franciscans, the Carmelites, the early Quakers, the Wesleyans—new life birthed out of terrible suffering. The Disciplines show us what to do to ground ourselves in God during stressful times.

Mimi: The spiritual Disciplines are the way our spiritual ancestors tethered themselves to God and to one another. In blizzard conditions, if any one of them were to slip into a crevasse, they were secure; they were tethered. They were not alone.

Nate: It isn't "just me and my rope"—

Mimi: That's right. This knowledge is what grounds my hope. Jesus is present among us as our ever-living Savior, Teacher, Lord, and Friend, and there is someone behind me and in front of me to help me keep going.

Nate: Yet we can't be there for each other if we don't know the stories. Is this what you mean, Dad, when you say, "Just be with people?"

Richard: Absolutely! Get to know the person—her stories, his experience of God. Just be *with* people.

Nate: I have a final question for you, Dad. The movement that *Celebration of Discipline* sparked introduced some new terms to the contemporary Christian lexicon: "spiritual Disciplines" and "spiritual formation." How do you feel about that?

Richard: I feel good about it so long as the meaning and the practice remain true.[170] And when it does, oh my, it's glory—the shekinah of God alive among us. Lives are formed and transformed in wonderful ways.

Mimi: It is the grace and goodness of God on display.

In our conversation today the three of us have touched upon the major themes and contributions that *Celebration of Discipline* has brought to the lives of individuals and entire communities of believers; we have imagined the future of the movement the book sparked. I wonder, Richard, would you offer a concluding word?

Richard: Sure! I will think on that and get back to you.

[A week later I received from Richard the following:]

We are seeking a life of flaming love for God with all our heart, soul, mind, and strength and to love our neighbor as ourselves. This is our first and last order of business. Nothing is more important. Nothing. Not good deeds. Not faithful service in the church. Not missional labor in the name of Christ. Nothing. We love God alone. We adore God alone. We worship God alone.

We are seeking to follow Jesus Christ at all times, in all places, and in all ways. He is our Savior to forgive us, our Teacher to guide us, our Lord to rule us, and our Friend to come alongside us.

We are seeking an ongoing, transformational character formation into Christlikeness. This involves an overall plan of living that includes the practice of spiritual Disciplines appropriate to our needs.

We are seeking to live in loving fellowship with other like-minded disciples of Jesus. This is to be an all-inclusive community of loving persons gathered in the power and fellowship of the Trinitarian presence.

We are seeking the common good in our culture and society by our words and deeds and way of life. We pray for and work toward justice and shalom upon the face of the earth.

Epilogue

You know, it's funny the way we tuck memories away, and we don't realize—we don't stop to reflect on what we have seen. But collecting people's testimonies in the assembly of this biography brought it all back. Writing the story of *Celebration of Discipline* has been a personal awakening.

I remember clearly the first day I met *Celebration of Discipline* in the Fuller Seminary bookstore. A quick scan of the contents presented the classic spiritual Disciplines as the means of God's grace for bringing about genuine personality formation characterized through and through by love and joy and peace and patience and kindness and goodness and faithfulness and gentleness and self-control (Galatians 5:22–23).[171] The book invited me into a life I longed to live.

Celebration of Discipline delivered on its promise. Practice of the Disciplines over the years has opened my eyes to recognize where and how God is at work so that I may cooperate more intentionally. Their practice has grounded me and provided safe passage through tumultuous storms. And, as if that were not enough, I've had a front row seat to the miraculous transformation that occurred when *Celebration of Discipline* landed in our church community. The corporate effect was the difference between a single lit candle and a roomful of burning candles. "When more than one or two people come into public worship with a holy expectancy," *Celebration* predicted, "it will change the atmosphere of the room. People who enter harried and distracted are drawn quickly into a sense of the quiet Presence. Hearts and minds are lifted upward. The very air becomes charged with expectancy." [172]

Social psychologists describe this as a "gestalt," where "the whole is greater than the sum of its individual parts." In worship, in fellowship, in group discussions, in business meetings, we discovered this principle at work. We "experienced more together" than any of us had on our own. As memories were healed, relationships restored, and lives were changed, there was a shared sense among us that Jesus was present to teach, to heal, and to guide. Like an army of caterpillars, we were slowly metamorphosing into a kaleidoscope of butterflies. It is a story worth celebrating; it was just—beautiful.

More than two millennia of experience has established the classical Disciplines of the spiritual life as a God-given means of grace to root individuals and entire communities in deep fellowship with the Trinity. They "call us to move beyond surface living into the depths. They invite us to explore the inner caverns of the spiritual realm." [173]

I hope that reading the story behind the story of *Celebration of Discipline* has piqued your curiosity and made you wonder, "Does this spiritual discipline stuff really work?" I assure you; it really does! It has for me. May you live into this reality for yourself.

Recommended Readings
in Spiritual Formation

Richard Foster did not invent the spiritual disciplines he described in *Celebration of Discipline* he mined them from the classic literature of the devotional masters. His purpose was to identify the twelve practices most accessible to contemporary Christians who are hungry for a deeper life with God.

In the fortieth anniversary edition of *Celebration of Discipline*, Richard identifies fifty books specifically related to spiritual formation that comprise, in his estimation, a canon for formation in Christlikeness.[174] He suggests that we begin, however, with a "Starter Kit" of twelve resources chosen from across the centuries. Richard lists these in the order they should be read—the first ones being the most accessible. The bibliographical information for each of the books is provided below, together with a brief descriptive word from me to help you get started. The point, Richard, emphasizes, is not *how many* of these books we read but *how much* of what we read we are able to draw into our own life experiences. Take it slow. Soak in what you read. Take your time.

147

Laubach, Frank. *Letters by a Modern Mystic*. Eastford, CT: Martino Fine Books, 2012.

A "mystic," refers to someone who believes that communication with God is actually possible—that it is possible to carry on a life-giving, life-altering conversation with our Creator! This little book, a favorite of mine, grew out of a particularly difficult period in Laubach's life where he felt he had failed entirely in his life's mission. He shares his intimate interactions with God around failure and loss, and the transformation of his soul that resulted.

Brother Lawrence. *The Practice of the Presence of God*. New York: Doubleday, 1977, Translated by John J. Delaney.

In 1978 Richard opened *Celebration of Discipline* with the declaration: "Superficiality is the curse of our age!" Today, he says, he would amend that statement to identify distraction as being the greatest burden we bear. It scatters our thinking and has a deleterious effect on every relationship. In this endearingly profound little book, Brother Lawrence shares how he developed, over time, the holy habit of simple attentiveness. He generously counsels us on how we may learn to keep our gaze upon God and walk constantly in God's presence even in the midst of our busy, fraught lives. For those of us caught in the cultural drift toward distraction, Brother Lawrence throws us a lifeline.

Athanasius of Alexandria. *The Life of Antony* and *The Letter to Marcellinlus*. New York: Paulist Press, 1980, Translated by Robert C. Cregg.

The story of Antonius, also known as Anthony, had a profound impact on Athanasius the Great, who was a renowned theologian, Church Father, defender of the faith, and noted Egyptian Christian leader of the fourth century. And no wonder! Antony's life of faith is a wonder and a marvel! He lived during a time when Christians were becoming increasingly secularized.

In his devotion to follow Jesus, Antony believed that somehow, Christians should be distinctive, they should live a life that is contagious with the love of God! So, he sold all he possessed and moved to the desert to engage fully the Disciplines of the spiritual life in single-minded devotion to Jesus. The stories Athanasius tells about the life of this humble, devoted disciple are inspiring and convicting. So striking was the transformation of Antony's life that simply by seeing his conduct, many aspired to become imitators of his way of life. You and I live in very different times, yet there is no question that the need for lives transformed into the character of Jesus is as great today as it ever has been. Perhaps greater. Antony is a wonderful teacher.

Woolman, John. *The Journal and Major Essays of John Woolman.* New York: Oxford University Press, 1971, Edited by Philips P. Moulton.

Over the years Richard Foster has become something of a student of John Woolman. He includes a rather lengthy discussion of Woolman in his doctoral dissertation, *Quaker Concern in Race Relations: Then and Now.* Richard demonstrates how instrumental Woolman was in bringing the Society of Friends (Quakers) to utterly reject human slavery even before the Declaration of Independence was signed. Woolman was deeply sensitive to issues of social justice that continue to plague our society and world: racism, consumerism, militarism, and more. Contemplating these, Woolman confided, "My mind is often led to consider the purity of the Divine Being, and the justice of his judgments; and herein my soul is covered with awfulness. The cries of the slaves have reached the ears of the Most High; now is not a time for delay!"[175] There are social implications, nay—social *imperatives* to our discipleship to Jesus. Friends, now is not a time to delay!

Lewis, C. S. *The Screwtape Letters*. San Francisco: HarperOne, 2015.

C. S. Lewis came up with the idea for *The Screwtape Letters* as he was leaving his church (Holy Trinity, Headington, England) following a Sunday service. The concept of the book is a senior devil, Screwtape, writing to his nephew, Wormwood, offering seasoned advice on how to be successful as a tempter. The book provides an imaginative, creative approach to our understanding of how the Enemy, Satan, chooses to approach followers of Jesus in a strategic campaign to deflect and distract and discourage. Entertaining as it is, Richard does not recommend that we spend too much time lingering with this particular book. Lewis himself confessed that writing it "produced a sort of spiritual cramp." Read it. Learn from it. Then move on to the next book in the Starter Kit!

Thomas a Kempis. *The Imitation of Christ*. Macon, Georgia, Mercer University Press, 1989, Translated by William C. Creasy.

The Imitation of Christ is a book to read and savor like a gumdrop dissolving slowly in your mouth. This little book has been the unchallenged devotional masterpiece since the fifteenth century, distilling the insights of a dynamic, conversational, relationship with Jesus that is so desperately needed in our own age and time. I suggest that you read *Imitation* in small bites, perhaps as a daily devotional over a period of time. It will feed your soul.

Kelly, Thomas. *A Testament of Devotion*. New York: HarperCollins, 1996.

I love this book! It is amazing, tantalizing, captivating, and dear. With beautiful imagery and deliciously evocative words, Kelly draws us into the subterranean chambers of our own soul offering a vision of what is possible in a deep, intimate relationship with Jesus. He shows us how to live from this center in a way that is simultaneously stabilizing and deeply contagious. I read and re-read this book on a regular basis.

Guyon, Jeanne. *Experiencing the Depths of Jesus Christ.* Translated by Gene Edwards. Sargent, GA: SeedSowers, 1975.

The simplicity of this devotional classic is stunning. Guyon herself said that she wrote it to induce the whole world to love God and to serve God in a way that is easier and simpler, it turns out, than any of us could imagine! The pages, born out of a profound experience of God, breathe with divine expectancy. Prayer, she says, is a melting! Prayer is a dissolving and an uplifting of the soul! Madam Guyon invites us to come, to join a conversation with Jesus that is occurring in this very moment.

Augustine of Hippo. *The Confessions of St. Augustine.* New York: Thomas Nelson Publishers, 1983, Translated by E. M. Blaiklock.

On his desk for years, my father had a framed quote from St. Augustine, "Thou hast made us for Thyself, and our heart shall find no rest till it rest in Thee" (now I have it on my desk). The *Confessions* tell the honest, vulnerable story of how a profligate young man came to faith in Jesus as his ever-living Savior, Teacher, Lord, and Friend. Outside of Scripture itself, Augustine's is the most famous conversion story in the Christian canon. The book is beautifully written and well, just wonderful. Jesus told Augustine, "Take and read." That advice applies well to this important book.

Doherty, Catherine de Hueck. *Poustinia: Encountering God in Silence, Solitude and Prayer.* 3rd ed. Combermere, Ontario: Madonna House Publications, 2000.

I was introduced to Doherty's *Poustinia* more than two decades ago on the Isle of Iona (located in the Inner Hebrides of Scotland). Jenny, the woman who hosted the guest house where I stayed, brought the book to me, recommending that I read it during my retreat. *Poustinia* (prounounced pow-stenia) is the Russian word for "desert." It describes an intentional withdrawl from society to be alone with Jesus in silence and solitude. For the next two weeks, the southern shore of Iona became my poustinia. Doherty rightly calls it "the place where heaven and earth meet," for as Jesus and I entered into an extended conversation our exchange had a transformative effect, shifting in significant ways both my thinking and my perspective. When my retreat ended, I brought poustinia home with me as a way to intentionally maintain the rhythm of life that had become so precious and restorative.

Willard, Dallas. *Renovation of the Heart: Putting on the Character of Christ*. Colorado Springs: NavPress, 2012.

Richard qualifies that all of Dallas Willard's books are important to read. He chose *Renovation* for this introductory short list because it provides an exceedingly thoughtful analysis of the human person: spirit (heart/will), mind (thought/feelings), body, social context, and soul. Willard's purpose is to help us understand how the human personality is actually formed, conformed, and transformed into the image of Christ. While Dallas Willard is no longer with us, his gentleness of soul and deep spiritual wisdom live on in his books, his teaching, and in the lives of all who had the privilege of knowing him. You are well served to immerse yourself in the writings of this humble servant and guide.

St. Teresa of Avila. *The Interior Castle*. Translated by Mirabai Starr. New York: Riverhead Book, 2003.

Dallas Willard and Richard Foster both cite *The Interior Castle* for providing the most thorough teaching on, and experience of, Christian prayer that is available. The book, in Richard's words, "positively dances with metaphor," presenting the soul as a castle whose central interior is approached through a progression of various movements. Teresa guides readers from the outermost rooms, room by room, further and further in, until we arrive at the innermost regions of the soul where the King has chosen to take up residency. Along the way, Teresa describes the different dynamics of the inward journey—what to expect, how it feels, the invitation into an increasing intimacy with Jesus, what is his work in the journey, what is ours. *The Interior Castle* can be complicated reading. But Renovaré recently guided readers in the Book Club through the *Castle* and resources are available to assist your exploration. I assure you it is well worth the effort!

This concludes Richard's Starter Kit of twelve resources. You might explore one book a month or choose to spend several months on a single book (my preferred approach). In any case, take your time. Soak in the wisdom of people from the past who navigated difficult times like ours with grace and power.

If you are looking for something a bit more curated to get started, you might consider these two resources that have been developed by our Renovaré team.

Devotional Classics edited by James Bryan Smith and Richard J. Foster, provides selections that are well recognized from the canon of devotional literature.[176]

Spiritual Classics edited by Emilie Griffin and Richard J. Foster, focuses attention on great writers of devotion that have been underrepresented, including women and people of color.[177]

Both collections will give you a taste of the writers mentioned in the Starter Kit, plus others. A particular reading might pique your curiosity to read more of the person whose story or words have caught your attention. In any case, get started! Have fun! Explore! Enjoy making acquaintance with some new old friends!

Letter to the Reader

—Richard J. Foster

Dear Reader,

I was thrilled when the idea emerged for me to add a "letter to the reader" as an afterword to this book project. Thrilled because it gave me the opportunity to say a huge "thank you" to you, the reader. You see, this work of spiritual formation can only go forward if there are many who take it up and make it their own. You, dear reader, have read and studied and prayed and lived into this life with God. You have teamed up with so many others around the world to think and dream and experience life with God.

When I first penned *Celebration of Discipline*, precious few were concerned about these matters. I felt like a lonely voice crying in the wilderness. However, just look at what is going on today! Books by the score are being written on the growth of the soul. Christian seminaries and colleges now provide courses and even majors in spiritual formation. Pastors in many places are teaching and guiding their people into life in the Kingdom of God. I know, I know—some of the books are shallow indeed, and some of the courses are merely exercises in academic futility, and some churches have succumbed to more soul-killing legalisms. Still, I thank God for all the good that has occurred, and the interest continues. You, dear reader, are a prime example of the life with God that is abounding in so many places.

So, thank you, dear reader, thank you, thank you, thank you. You encourage me more than you will ever know. The Kingdom of God is making significant inroads through your work and your study and your life. I thank God for you.

Now, I would like to provide one simple counsel as you go forward in this with-God life. How about us making our lives one grand experiment in bringing holiness and hilarity together in one life-giving unity! Let's combine seeking after God with an ease and lightheartedness in our spirituality. Maybe even levity and freedom of spirit.

This combination of a life focused on the divine Center with a lighthearted spirituality is seldom seen in our day. It is an occupational hazard of religious folk to become stuffy bores. So, perhaps we can relax a bit and enjoy being present with God. Maybe we can even have a good belly laugh at ourselves whenever we get too intense!

I don't mean this in an outward or showy way. We need not "try" to be joyful. Instead, we simply invite God to produce deep within us a well of life bubbling up and flowing out. We can ask to experience a deep river of divine intimacy, a gentle river of holy living, a dancing river of jubilation in the Spirit, and a broad river of unconditional love for all people. Such a river of life will surely draw others in.

* * *

Last night while I was contemplating this letter to you, I fell asleep. At least I think I was asleep—although I continued thinking about my letter to you. Anyway, in my dream (or perhaps in my imagination for I am not sure whether I was awake or asleep), I "saw" something that startled me. What I saw was the seeping wound of the human soul.

I was transfixed, staring at this festering wound. In this wound I could feel the pain, the sorrow, and the tears of so many.

"Who is this?" I asked of the Lord.

The response was instant, "This is every woman. This is every man. This is you, Richard. This is you, dear reader. This is the human condition."

"Can the wound ever be healed?" I questioned.

"Oh yes!" The reply was immediate and joy-filled. "This *is* the work of the formation and conformation and transformation of the human life. For some, healing will be instantaneous, for others long and torturous. But in either case, a scar will remain. This will remind you of your humanity, your frailty, your utter dependence upon me."

With that, my dream (or perhaps my waking vision) ended. I opened my eyes. It was 5 a.m.

Well, dear reader, we *are* wounded human beings. No doubt, our wounds are in different places, but each and every one of us carries wounds of one kind or another. So, may I urge us to be tender with one another as our soul wounds are being healed. Just like we rejoice with those who rejoice, we also learn to weep with those who weep. Remember, the divine Son of Man weeps with us. Jesus is our Savior to forgive us. Jesus is our Teacher to guide us. Jesus is our Lord to rule us. Jesus is our Friend to come alongside us.

I close this letter to you, dear reader, with a blessing, an ancient blessing, sometimes called "the Aaronic blessing." It is recorded for us in Numbers 6:24–26.

> The Lord bless you and keep you;
> > the Lord make his face to shine upon you,
> > and be gracious to you;
> The Lord lift up his countenance upon you,
> > and give you peace.

Peace and joy,
Richard J. Foster

Acknowledgments

First, I give thanks to God, who makes transformation in Christ possible! I next have a number of people to thank for their part in bringing this biography to publication. I am particularly grateful to Roy M. Carlisle who brought the idea of a book biography to Richard J. Foster in the first place. And I am grateful to our little team, composed of Roy, Richard, Nathan Foster, my brilliant literary agent Kathryn Helmers, and my friend and colleague Deborah Rillos. This book is better for the suggestions and input of each team member, and, especially, for the generous contributions of Richard himself. Not every book biography has the benefit of consultation with the original author; Richard has been exceedingly generous in his support.

I thank Carolynn Foster, Carolyn Arends, James Catford, Dwight Dixon, Lyle Smith-Graybeal, and Chris Hall for their assistance at critical junctures, and Margaret Campbell, Richella Parham, and the Renovaré Ministry Team for praying me through the project during the long seclusion of COVID-19. I thank Jean and David Nevills for their generous hospitality when I was conducting research in the Richard Foster archives at George Fox University. I am deeply grateful to the many people who willingly responded to interviews I conducted via Zoom, and, especially, to Lynda Graybeal, Richard's longtime Associate. Lynda deserves special acknowledgment, because during the late 1970s and 1980s she collected book reviews, sales reports, articles, and interviews about *Celebration of Discipline* that she then packed into boxes and shipped to me. She was, to all intents and purposes, my research assistant. Thank you, Lynda, for saving everything in your treasure-trove collection.

At the heart of this biography are a plethora of individual testimonies. The year *Celebration of Discipline* marked its fortieth anniversary, Richard and Nathan Foster conducted a ten-city tour offering grateful readers the opportunity to gather and submit comments about their experience of the book. Quite a number of these found their way into the pages of the biography. You know who you are; thank you!

At the end of the day, this book is in your hands due to the foresight and courage of Eric Muhr at Barclay Press. Book biographies are unusual and new enough that there is not yet an established category for this kind of publication. Eric Muhr and Barclay Press saw this book's potential and have taken the risk of publishing in an untried and new field; I thank them.

Finally, I thank those of you who love *Celebration of Discipline* and purchased this biography to learn the story behind the story. I hope you have enjoyed reading it as much as I enjoyed writing it! You are the true heroes. The transformative influence of the spiritual Disciplines in your lives launched a movement of growth in Christlikeness that has shaped an entire generation of Christians. It makes me wonder whether, in our current era of instability and white-out conditions, *Celebration of Discipline* is poised to deliver its deepest impact yet on the next generation of Christ-followers. My fervent prayer is, *may it be so.*

APPENDIX A

Book Reviews,
Published Citations,
Other Publications

Book sales are commonly held as being the most reliable, quantifiable means to track the career of a book. Sales are driven by book reviews, where the qualifications of the author are presented along with an overview of their main points. The reviewer provides an opinion as to whether the author succeeds in convincing readers of their message. Taken as a whole, book reviews in the United States uniformly endorsed *Celebration of Discipline* for its content and style. What follows is a sampling of those reviews.

QUAKER REVIEWS

George Fox College President David Le Shana:

The perceptions of Richard Foster are both timely and profound. *Celebration of Discipline* is scholarly yet warm and sincere as it encourages the reader to discover the reality and joy of spiritual maturity through a disciplined life. Foster has written *Quaker Concern in Race Relations: Then and Now,* published in 1970 and numerous magazine articles; he also speaks at various camps and conferences. This year he was honored as "Writer of the Year." I am grateful for the insight Foster has shared with us.[178]

Florence Lawson, Quaker periodical Palladium-Item*:*

This first book by a young Friends pastor, Richard J. Foster, is about his experiments in the practical application of classical Christian Disciplines to modern-day living. Foster visualizes the Disciplines as "stepping-stones" along the path to inner growth. If the author of books on practical religion doesn't write something "an ordinary person" can respond to, his work will simply sit in bookstores. That is the key to success in religious book writing, says Richard J. Foster, 37, author of *Celebration of Discipline*, published in June last year. Roughly 15,000 copies have been sold, and the book currently ranks third among the top 10 religious books on Harper & Row's bestseller list.[179]

Jack L. Wilcuts, The Friend*:*

Richard Foster bursts out of evangelical anonymity to startle the Christian community with a whole heartful of new insights. Fresh, dynamic, provocative, scholarly, done in a style as contemporary as *Time* magazine, *Celebration of Discipline* lifts one to the turf of saints, a view of what Christianity is meant to be and always has been. He tackles touchy subjects head-on—healing, fasting, simple lifestyle, prayer, meditation—and opens his heart as a competent acquaintance with the devotional classics in an extraordinary way. One reads (savors?) a chapter at a time.[180]

Hart Armstrong, For Defenders Friends*:*

Celebration of Discipline, by Dr. Richard J. Foster, delivers more than it promises. . . . Basing his thought in the Scriptures and in the tradition of great spiritual thinkers of the past, such as George Fox, Thomas á Kempis, Francis of Assisi, and Thomas Kelly, Dr. Foster stakes out a path of his own original thought in guiding the reader to a solid, passable road which leads to a deeper inner life, and to an experience of overwhelming joy in Christ.[181]

CHURCH OF THE BRETHREN

Timothy K. Jones, Quarterly Review:

The Quaker writer and teacher Richard Foster argues in *Celebration of Discipline* that faith must move beyond superficiality and the "doctrine of instant satisfaction." The need in our world is "not for a greater number of intelligent people, or gifted people, but for deep people." Spiritual disciplines call us to "move beyond surface living into the depths." Foster's unmistakable debt to Quaker thought enriches rather than impoverishes, for he has drawn freely at the wells of Protestants and Catholic, as well.[182]

METHODIST

Paul L. Morell, Good News Magazine:

Celebration of Discipline has become widely acclaimed. It is a timely book for United Methodists and others who wish to grasp the direction and possibilities of spiritual formation. Across our denomination many are waking up to the widespread neglect—even ignorance—of spiritual habits that encourage Christ-like growth. The author is not a United Methodist but a Quaker. Because he is true to the traditional Quaker concerns about the inner life, however, United Methodists can gain much that complements our own Wesleyan perspective. The author often quotes John Wesley, for Methodism's founder remains a mountaineer of the holy life.[183]

EPISCOPALIAN

Bishop William C. Fry, writes:

Too often the spiritual Disciplines are thought to be reserved either for the spiritual giants or for those privileged souls who do not have to cope with the "distractions" of a family or a full-time job. Richard Foster rescues the Disciplines from the specialists and the ascetics and returns them to the ordinary disciples for whom they are intended. His vision of a "disciple in training" embraces both the assembly-line worker and the academic, the harried mother of small children, the office worker, and the cleric.[184]

SEVENTH DAY ADVENTIST

Peter Prime in the Adventist Review:

Some may ask if these Disciplines are compatible with the gospel of grace, or if they are legalistic. Foster adeptly explains how the Disciplines affirm the integrity of the gospel of grace rather than deny it. The Disciplines are not about the Disciplines per se. They are about God. By themselves, they carry no intrinsic redemptive and transformational value. They are rather like the fig tree without fruit and the cloud without moisture that offer nothing but empty promises. Accordingly, the Disciplines must be treated, not as ends in themselves but as channels through which the riches of God's grace may flow uninterruptedly. What is particularly impressive is the author's understanding of the role of spiritual Disciplines in the context of the gospel of grace and their application to Christian maturity.[185]

ROMAN CATHOLIC

Roman Catholic Christians gave *Celebration of Discipline* a warm reception. Scottish theologian Thomas Smail said, "The rich unity that God has for us consists in the fellowship of Roman Christians, Anglican Christians, Baptist Christians, Pentecostal Christians, and the rest who have not left their treasures behind them, but who have purified and made their own what God gave to their fathers and now come to give and to receive across all the breached barriers of the past."[186] Barriers which had existed for centuries were disappearing as believers found common meeting ground. Entire chapters were reproduced in Catholic periodicals, encouraging their readers to read and digest *Celebration of Discipline.*

JESUIT

The primary requirement and motivating principle behind the steady practice of the Disciplines is the longing for God. The purpose of the Disciplines is to put us where God can work within us and transform us. *Celebration of Discipline* can be recommended to all who are seeking to deepen their life in the Spirit.[187]

THE SAN FRANCISCO CATHOLIC

Celebration of Discipline is a straightforward, insightful treatment of the traditional aids to spiritual growth (meditation, fasting, prayer, study, direction, celebration), deeply grounded in Scripture and the classics of spirituality, yet written in practical, direct contemporary language and out of the author's own experience.[188]

SISTERS TODAY

This is indeed a choice volume to be read fruitfully by every Christian, whatever her/his denomination of faith. In clear, definite easy style, the author, an exemplary Quaker, spells out the "path to spiritual growth," the way to a "free spirit" via the road of discipline. Even the *Finis* is a scholarly, succinct overview of the work's comprehensive content, whose depth moves the reader (in the words of St. Paul in his letter to the Philippians 3:14) "to press on toward the goal for the prize of the upward call of God in Christ Jesus" (p.171).[189]

Several reviewers noted apparent omissions to the text. In Foster's chapter on worship, several expressed surprise that there was no mention of the sacraments. Another reviewer remarked that as the author is a Quaker, he expected Foster's chapter on service to place a greater emphasis on social action. A British reviewer dryly commented that regardless of Foster's obvious enthusiasm for his subject, application of the word "celebration" to any discussion of discipline was optimistic at best.

As was typical of domestic reviews, the international response to *Celebration of Discipline* was uniformly positive.

CANADIAN REVIEW

Alan Cadwallader, Anglican Vicar of St. Georges in Flemington, Victoria, wrote, "Richard Foster comes from a tradition which inculcates a sensitivity to the Spirit—he is a Quaker—and seems to have built his handbook for others on a foundation of his personal pilgrimage. His insights are too profound to be other than tried in the fire of his own experience—from his exposition of the captivity wrought by and evidenced in a propensity to justify oneself, to the helpful place of fasting in one's spiritual growth."[190]

BRITISH REVIEWS OF
THE HODDER & STOUGHTON EDITION

Church of England newspaper wrote, "This reprint of *Celebration of Discipline* from America presents language problems, but they are well worth overcoming for this is a book which must make us pause. How far are we training our congregations in prayer, and how far are we really growing ourselves? Here you will find a rich mine of treasure."[191]

Jeffrey M. Young, writing for the *Herald*, observed, "I often notice a distinct difference between the time I spend in worship every week and the rest of my day-to-day life. Our society tends to reinforce this difference by telling us that a certain time each week is for 'religion,' while other times are for 'work,' 'entertainment,' 'family activities,' and so on. Wouldn't it be great to be able to carry some of the spiritual depth of worship over into the rest of your life? Richard Foster's book, *Celebration of Discipline*, tells us how to do that. It is a book that will change your life. It will show you how to get out of the way and allow God to change your life."[192]

THE FRIEND

"In a permissive do-as-you-please age, 'discipline' is not a very popular word, and the *Celebration of Discipline* seems a contradiction in terms. Yet this book may persuade us that Discipline isn't any stuffy, kill-joy obedience to rules: rather, it calls for an inside job—a transforming spirit within us that is accompanied by the festivity, dance, and song of the Kingdom. Here is a fresh treatment about the cultivation of the inner life. . . . Our greatest problems are not social, economic, political or technological; they are moral and spiritual, and this book is a welcome contribution to the cultivation of the life of the spirit."[193]

EVANGELICAL QUARTERLY

"When so many paperbacks are merely run-of-the-mill, ordinary, with little that is really original to say, it is stimulating to come across one which breaks some new ground. Richard Foster is a Quaker who writes out of the dual conviction that 'superficiality is the curse of our age' and that the classical spiritual Disciplines can lead us 'beyond surface living into the depths.'

'We must always remember that the path does not produce the change; it only puts us in the place where the change can occur.' One can do no better than endorse the conclusion of David Watson's foreword: 'I warmly commend *Celebration of Discipline* for thoughtful study, prayer and application.'"[194]

RESTORATION

"There are things we can and must do; God cannot, and will not, do them for us. These depend on the inner attitude of the heart for their success. . . . *Celebration of Discipline* has a flavour of Tozer about it, which is high praise and must be a recommendation to many."[195]

THE CHURCHMAN

"There is a sturdy Christian realism about *Celebration of Discipline* which should help many people to understand better what is happening to them when God leads them into times of (for example) spiritual darkness and quiescence or calls them to more vigorous activity in the things of the Spirit. This is a balanced account of the spiritual pilgrimage, replete with much biblically grounded advice for the Christian pilgrim."[196]

BRITISH CHURCH TIMES

"Only occasionally will an Anglican recollect that this author is a Quaker. . . . Ecumenism is certainly producing its fruit; and, since the source from which all Christians come is the same, the tendency to convergence must always assert itself. A foreword by David Watson 'warmly commends' *Celebration of Discipline*. So will all who read it."[197]

Australian Reviews

Evangel Magazine

"*Celebration of Discipline* calls Christians to go beyond superficiality—a mark of our society. The spiritual Disciplines can lead to the area or attitude in one's life where God can work from within and therefore bring about a transformation. This book is obviously the product of prayer, research, observation—a mature work for those who yearn to go deeper in God. Recommended reading."[198]

Australian Church Record

"*Celebration of Discipline* is inspired by the Bible, the Great Fathers, Augustine, the Medieval mystics, Puritans and modern masters like Bonhoeffer. It doesn't split the spiritual off into some other stratosphere separate from earthly life but is commendably wholistic in its approach to worshiping in the world. I found the book to be of great help and commend it."[199]

Published Citations

Positive book reviews and enthusiastic recommendations by readers drove the sales of *Celebration of Discipline* through the ceiling. It was not long before the book literally "took on a life of its own" and was cited in newspaper articles, magazine articles, periodicals, and books. The following are some examples of published citations.

- *Christianity Today* cited *Celebration of Discipline* in a January 7, 1983, article entitled, "The Ministry of the Towel: Practicing Love through Service."[200]
- Dr. Siang-Yang Tan, professor of clinical psychology at Fuller Theological Seminary, cited Richard Foster's *Celebration of Discipline* in six of his books: *Lay Counseling* (1991), *Disciplines of the Holy Spirit* (1997), *Rest* (2000),

Full Service (2006), *Counseling and Psychotherapy: A Christian Perspective* (2011; 2020), *Shepherding God's People: A Guide to Faithful and Fruitful Pastoral Ministry* (2019).

- *Christianity Today* cited *Celebration of Discipline* in a January 8, 1993, issue.
- *Celebration of Discipline* was cited in *Intimacy with God* by John Caldwell, published by College Press in 1995:

   "Richard Foster has written what is to me the finest book on Christian disciplines of this century, *Celebration of Discipline*."

- Journalist Mark Oppenheimer, in an article for the *New York Times* titled, "Many Choices on the Menu of Religious Fasts," told the story of a woman's introduction to the spiritual Discipline of fasting through reading *Celebration of Discipline*:

   Ms. McElroy, 27, is subsisting for three weeks on just water. "I first did a water fast last year, after reading about it in *Celebration of Discipline*, by Richard Foster. The minute I read it, I knew that's what God wanted me to do," Ms. McElroy said. When we spoke, she was on Day 8. Saying the discipline of fasting helps clarify God's intentions for her, she pointed to Matthew 17, where Jesus recommends prayer and fasting to His disciples. But she does not say fasting is easy. "In those moments when I think, 'Okay, God, I can't do this,' I rely on His strength. I have no temptation because I know why I'm doing it."[201]

- Editors Nicola Hoggard Creegan and Andrew Shepherd cited *Celebration of Discipline* in a Pickwick publication titled *Creation and Hope*:

   "Richard Foster urges that in the face of 'abysmal ignorance,' there must be a renewal of classic spiritual

Disciplines if the enjoyment of Sabbath is not to become mere indulgence, and the resting of Sabbath not crushing boredom. Consumers must become contemplatives."[202]

- The periodical *Liberal Education* cited *Celebration of Discipline* in an article titled, "Religion on Campus."[203] The article asserted that students today are more likely to ask, "Where do I meet God?" than to ponder the question, "Does God exist?"

- A May 2005 cover article written by Lauren Winner for *Christianity Today* quotes *Celebration of Discipline* in her promotion of chastity as a spiritual Discipline:

    "The language of spiritual discipline, an ancient idiom of the church, has come into vogue again. In the 1970s and '80s, two books on spiritual disciplines, now rightly considered modern-day classics, were published: Richard Foster's *Celebration of Discipline* and Dallas Willard's *The Spirit of the Disciplines*. Foster and Willard called readers to deepen their Christian lives by incorporating ancient practices of the church. These books struck a tremendous chord, and Christians of all stripes began exploring habits and structures like liturgical prayer, fasting, solitude, simplicity, and tithing."[204]

- Australian author Katherine Thompson cites *Celebration of Discipline* in her book titled, *Christ Centred Mindfulness*:

    "The twentieth century saw a reawakening of interest in Christian contemplative prayer and meditation. This occurred first in Catholicism and then spread to Protestantism. What is even more interesting is that at the start of the twenty-first century, we began seeing the spiritual disciplines and contemplative prayer strategies come into mainstream evangelicalism. This change was most probably a reaction against the emphasis on rational thought that is a core value of modernity, and because a postmodern worldview makes people more open to explore new ways of expressing faith. It addresses the weakness of focusing only on thinking and knowledge, as these things alone cannot produce the necessary transformation that is essential to being a follower of Christ. An emphasis on spiritual disciplines has been championed by Richard Foster, Dallas Willard, John Ortberg, and James Bryan Smith. These disciplines and practices have become popular because there has been a growing awareness of the lack of integration between our knowledge about God and our connection to God."[205]

- In 2013, Ken Shigematsu cited *Celebration of Discipline* twice in his book *God in My Everything*. On page 55, "Richard Foster says 'of all the spiritual disciplines, prayer is the most central because it ushers us into perpetual communion with the Father.'" On page 131, "Richard Foster says, 'More than any other discipline, fasting reveals the things that control us.'"[206]

Additional citations:

- Howard Baker, *Soul Keeping: Ancient Paths of Spiritual Direction* and *The One True Thing*[207]
- Ruth Haley Barton cites *Celebration of Discipline* as a source in *Invitation to Silence and Solitude*, and in Appendix C of *Sacred Rhythms*[208]
- David Benner, *Sacred Companions*[209]
- Adele Ahlberg Calhoun includes *Celebration of Discipline* in the bibliography of *Spiritual Disciplines Handbook*[210]
- Peter Greig, *The Vision and the Vow*[211]
- Valerie E. Hess offers *Celebration of Discipline* as a recommended resource in *Spiritual Disciplines Devotional*[212]
- Jan Johnson, *Spiritual Disciplines Companion*[213]
- M. Robert Mulholland Jr., *Invitation to a Journey*[214]

- John Ortberg, *The Life You've Always Wanted* and *Soul Keeping*[215]
- James Bryan Smith's Apprentice series, *The Good and Beautiful God; The Good and Beautiful Life; The Good and Beautiful Community*[216]
- Dallas Willard, *The Divine Conspiracy*[217]

For years running, selections and entire chapters from *Celebration of Discipline* were reprinted in periodicals, magazines, and booklets representing nearly every Protestant denomination, Roman Catholic, and Christian organization worldwide.

In the early 1980s, when Richard was teaching at Friends University, Gateway produced and released a four-part film series covering the concepts contained in *Celebration of Discipline*:

- *Spiritual Discipline: The Door to Liberation.*
- *The Inward Disciplines.*
- *The Outward Disciplines.*
- *The Corporate Disciplines.*[218]

A SAMPLING OF PUBLICATIONS INFLUENCED BY *CELEBRATION OF DISCIPLINE*

Former Harper Editor Roy M. Carlisle contends that *Celebration of Discipline* almost singlehandedly began to change the course of evangelical religious publishing as the book's enthusiastic reception encouraged the publication of similar books. "*Celebration of Discipline* opened a door, many doors, to a deeper spirituality that was not based on just trying harder—the bane of most evangelical spirituality."[219]

Lyle Smith-Graybeal agrees: "*Celebration of Discipline* reintroduced Christians to our spiritual history and opened the way for a kind of writing that pointed to Jesus and highlighted the intentional rhythm of life that he practiced and that generations of his disciples have since embraced. Spiritual formation in Christ has become a common theme in subsequent publications."[220]

When queried about which subsequent publications were inspired by *Celebration of Discipline,* Lyle Smith-Graybeal, Richard Hovey, and Jan Johnson suggested the following titles:

- Ruth Haley Barton: *Sacred Rhythms: Arranging Our Lives for Spiritual Transformation; Invitation to Silence and Solitude: Experiencing God's Transforming Presence; Invitation to Retreat: The Gift and Necessity of Time Away with God*
- Kyle David Bennett, *Practices of Love: Spiritual Disciplines for the Life of the World*
- Adele Calhoun, *Spiritual Disciplines Handbook: Practices that Transform Us*
- Barry Callen, *Authentic Spirituality: Moving Beyond Mere Religion*
- Nathan Foster, *The Making of an Ordinary Saint*
- Jan Johnson, *Invitation to the Spiritual Life*
- Tony Jones, *The Sacred Way*
- James Earl Massey, *Spiritual Disciplines: A Believer's Openings to the Grace of God*
- Robert Mulholland Jr., *Invitation to a Journey: A Road Map for Spiritual Transformation*
- John Ortberg, *The Life You've Always Wanted: Spiritual Disciplines for Ordinary People*
- Peter Scazzero, *Emotionally Healthy Spirituality*
- James Bryan Smith's *Apprentice* series
- Siang Yang Tan, *Disciplines of the Holy Spirit, Rest, Full Service, Disciplines of the Holy Spirit: How to Connect to the Spirit's Power and Presence*
- Gary Thomas, *Authentic Faith*
- Marjorie Thompson, *Soul Feast*
- Donald Whitney, *Spiritual Disciplines for the Spiritual Life*
- Jim Wilder, *Renovated*
- Dallas Willard, *The Spirit of the Disciplines*

Celebration of Discipline triggered a veritable avalanche of subsequent publications like these, reinforcing the significance of Richard's seminal work. Listed under the category of "Christian Spiritual Formation," Amazon.com currently offers over 8,000 volumes, any one of which might trace its spiritual lineage directly or indirectly back to *Celebration of Discipline*.

Appendix B

About Richard Foster, Publications

Richard J. Foster studied at George Fox College and received a Doctor of Pastoral Theology from Fuller Theological Seminary. Over the years Richard has served as a pastor, taught at universities and seminaries, and spoken worldwide on spiritual formation. Author of over sixty articles and six bestselling books, including *Celebration of Discipline*, hailed by many as the best modern book on Christian spirituality, Richard continues to write on the spiritual life. He and his wife, Carolynn, have two grown children, Joel and Nathan, nine grandchildren, and live near Denver, Colorado.

All of the editions of the books
Richard has written.

RICHARD FOSTER PUBLICATIONS

- *Celebration of Discipline*–1978, 1988 (revised and expanded), 1998, 2018.
- Study Guide for *Celebration of Discipline*, 1982.
- *Freedom of Simplicity*, 1982—recipient of the Gold Medallion and Christy Book Awards (revised edition 2005).
- *The Challenge of the Disciplined Life: Christian Reflections on Money, Sex, and Power*, 1985.
- Study Guide to *Money, Sex, and Power*, 1985.
- *Celebrating the Disciplines* with Kathyrn Yanni, 1992.
- Leader's Guide for *Freedom of Simplicity*, 1993.
- *Prayer: Finding the Heart's True Home*—winner of the Gold Medallion Book Award, 1993.
- *Coming Home: An Invitation to Prayer*, 1993.
- *Devotional Classics,* co-edited with James Bryan Smith, 1993.
- *Prayers from the Heart*, 1994.
- *Seeking the Kingdom*, 1995.
- *Prayer Treasury* (including *Prayer* and *Prayers from the Heart*), 1996.
- *Treasure of Christian Discipline* (includes *Celebration of Discipline, The Challenge of the Disciplined Life*, and *Freedom of Simplicity*), 1996.
- *Streams of Living Water: Celebrating the Great Traditions of Christian Faith*—1999 Gold Medallion Book Award, 1999.
- *Spiritual Classics,* co-edited with Emilie Griffin, 1999.
- *The Renovaré Spiritual Formation Bible*, 2005.
- *Sanctuary of the Soul: Journey into Meditative Prayer*, 2011.
- *Learning Humility: A Year of Searching for a Vanishing Virtue*, 2022.

The Renovaré Vision

The Renovaré Vision is simple and straightforward: a life of flaming love for God with all our "heart, soul, mind, and strength" and to love our neighbor as ourselves (Mark 12:29–31).

It is a vision of genuine, solid, substantive life in the Kingdom of God, available to all. Here. Now.

It is a vision of the continuing, experiential reality of "righteousness and peace and joy in the Holy Spirit" (Romans 14:17).

It is a vision of right love, right desire, and right passion rooted and grounded in God.

It is a vision of Jesus high and lifted up, drawing all peoples to himself and to his work here on Earth (John 3:14).

It is a vision of us constantly returning to our first love, Jesus, and falling in love with him over and over and over again (Revelation 2:4–5). It is a vision of an ongoing forming, conforming, transforming life in and through Jesus—a transformational character development into Christlikeness.

It is a vision of radical, life-giving community life; an all-inclusive community of loving persons gathered in the power and fellowship of the Trinitarian presence.

This is a vision of life. For all persons, at all times, in all places. We are never to leave off pursuing this life. Though it be difficult, we seek hard after it. And in the seeking, we are transformed into people who can learn to love God with all of our heart and soul and mind and strength. We can learn to love our neighbor as ourselves. We can learn to love our enemies. We can learn to overcome evil with good. We can learn to do what is right. We can learn these things. Renovaré is committed to helping people everywhere find just such a life.

To be sure, this life is not automatic, though God bestows innumerable graces upon the earnest seeker. Still, developing and sustaining a life of loving abandonment to God involves an overall plan of living, incorporating special practices that care for the inner person. These are the familiar Disciplines of the spiritual life. These we put into regular practice: prayer and solitude and study and service and worship and confession and celebration and more.

Through all of the vicissitudes of life, we must never allow anything to replace this vision of white-hot love for God. It is our first and our last order of business. Nothing is more important than this. Nothing. Not good deeds. Not faithful service in the church. Not missional labor in the name of Christ. Nothing. We love God alone. We adore God alone. We worship God alone.[221]

Appendix D

Definition of Christian Spiritual Formation

Christian spiritual formation is the process of being shaped by the Spirit into the likeness of Christ, filled with love for God and the world.

God calls us all to become like Jesus. Jesus says, "I have come that they may have life, and have it abundantly." We experience this abundance of life—here and now—as our passions, character, understanding, and relationships are increasingly aligned with those of Christ. This lifelong transformation within and among us is the continual gift of God's Spirit. We are called to be renewed into the likeness of Jesus—but we do not always fully embrace this calling. Sometimes we seem content to be known as "Christians" without intentionally engaging with this work of the Holy Spirit in our lives. Other times we desperately long for a new way of life, wanting to grow in our walk with Jesus, but needing help and encouragement. We, therefore, commit to pursue passionately and to receive joyfully God's grace to be more fully transformed into the image of Jesus Christ.

John 7:37–39; John 10:10; Romans 8:29; I Corinthians
11:1; I Corinthians 15:49; II Corinthians 3:17–18;
II Corinthians 4:16–18; II Corinthians 5:16–21;
Galatians 4:19; Ephesians 1:3; Ephesians 3:16–19; I
John 3:2; I John 4:17

As we are rooted in Jesus and in the Kingdom he proclaims,
we are progressively transformed. Jesus is the center of all life
and history, both the source and goal of all creation. God shaped
this universe as a place where the love and life of Jesus Christ
might flourish. Because we are formed in the divine image,
we have the capacity to receive and express this life and love.
Although human disobedience corrupts the divine image in us,
God still forms a people able to love the Lord their God with all
their heart, soul, mind, and strength, and love their neighbors
as themselves. Jesus makes this possible through his life, death,
and resurrection. In him, we experience a restored relationship
of love with God and one another and continual transformation
into his likeness. We are becoming a reconciled and renewed
community—which is both the goal and the substance of life in
God's Kingdom. This the good news we proclaim with joy to
the whole world.

Genesis 1:26–28; Genesis 3:1–7; Proverbs 8:22–31;
Isaiah 42:5–9; Jeremiah 31:33–34; Mark 12:28–
34; John 1:1–18; John 13:34–35; Romans 5:9–11;
Romans 8:1–11; Romans 8:19–23; Ephesians 2:11–
22; Colossians 1:9–23; I Thessalonians 5:23; I John
2:7–11

Our engagement with God's transforming grace is vital.
Renewal into the image of Christ is not a human attainment; it
is a gift of grace. God mercifully uses all our experiences, including our suffering and trials, to teach and transform us. Even so,
transformation requires our involvement and effort. We need to
make ourselves available to the Holy Spirit's work in all our life
experiences, particularly through intentional engagement with
historical Christian Disciplines, including Word and sacrament.

These practices open us to the presence and grace of God. As a result, we become, through time and experience, the kind of persons who naturally express love, joy, peace, patience, kindness, goodness, faithfulness, gentleness, and self-control.

> Matthew 5:43–48; Matthew 11:29–30; Luke 6:40; John 7:38; John 15:5–17; Romans 12:1–2; Galatians 5:16–25; Philippians 2:12–13; Philippians 3:12–16; Titus 2:11–14; Hebrews 5:13–6:1; Hebrews 12:7–13; James 4:7–8; I Peter 2:2; I Peter 4:1–2

Spiritual formation happens in community. As we long to know and follow Jesus and be formed into his likeness, we journey with those who share this longing. God is calling the church to be a place of transformation. Here we struggle to fulfill our calling to love. Here we learn to attend to the invitations of God's Spirit. Here we follow the presence of God in our midst. Spiritual community is the catalyst for our transformation and a sending base for our mission of love to the world.

> Matthew 18:20; Luke 6:12–19; John 17:20–26; Acts 2:42–47; Romans 12:4–8; I Corinthians 12:1–7; Galatians 6:1–2; Ephesians 4:1–16; Hebrews 10:23–25; I Peter 2:4–10

Spiritual formation is, by its very nature, missional. As we are formed into the likeness of Christ, we increasingly share God's infinitely tender love for others. We deepen in our compassion for the poor, the broken, and the lost. We ache and pray and labor for others in a new way, a selfless way, a joy-filled way. Our hearts are enlarged toward all people and toward all of creation.

> Isaiah 60:1–4; Matthew 5:14–16; Matthew 28:18–20; John 3:16–21; John 20:21–23; II Corinthians 5:20; Galatians 6:10; I John 4:7–21

We invite all people, everywhere, to embrace with us this calling to become like Jesus. By God's grace, we will seek to become lovers: lovers of God, lovers of people, and lovers of all creation. We will immerse ourselves in a lifestyle that is attentive and responsive to the gracious presence of God. We commit ourselves to the community of Christ's beloved, the church, so that we can learn this way of love together. We entreat you to join us.

Matthew 5:1–10; Matthew 13:44–46; Mark 1:15;
Luke 9:23–24; Romans 12:1–2; II Corinthians 6:1;
I Timothy 6:11–12; Revelation 21:2; Revelation 22:17

NOTE: 200 scholars, authors, and leaders in spiritual formation reviewed and approved this definition of Christian Spiritual Formation. At the Renovaré International Conference in San Antonio in 2009, it was formally adopted. This document has since been signed by hundreds of Christians, asserting their agreement of the need for careful attention to spiritual formation.

The Danger of Spiritual Disciplines

Seven Pitfalls to Avoid

Richard J. Foster

In *The Imitation of Christ,* Thomas à Kempis says, "The life of a good man must be mighty in virtues, that he should be inwardly what he appears outwardly to others." We need God's life and light to transform our inner spirit so that righteousness, peace, and joy in the Holy Spirit begin to pervade all we are and think. But such purity of heart does not just fall on our heads. We need to go through a process of sowing to the Spirit, through the exercise of the classical Disciplines of the spiritual life. As Elizabeth O'Connor has said, "No person or group or movement has vigor and power unless it is disciplined." We must take up a consciously chosen course of action that places us before God in such a way that he can work the righteousness of the Kingdom into us.

These Spiritual Disciplines concern both group and individual life. They include both inward and outward experiences. Through *meditation,* we come to hear God's voice and obey his word. *Prayer* is the life of perpetual communion. *Fasting* is one means through which we open our spirits to the Kingdom of God and concentrate upon the work of God. Through the spiritual experience of *study,* the mind takes on the order and rhythm of whatever it concentrates upon. These inward disciplines are joined by outward disciplines. *Simplicity*, the life characterized by singleness of purpose, sets us free from the tyranny of ourselves, the tyranny of other people, and the tyranny of material possessions. *Solitude* invites us to enter the recreating silences and let go of our inner compulsions. Through the liberating discipline of *submission*, we can lay aside the burden of always needing to get our own way. In *service*, we can experience the many little deaths of going beyond ourselves that, in the end, bring resurrection and life. Finally, disciplined living also includes important corporate experiences. *Confession* is that gracious provision of God through which the wounds of sin may be healed. *Worship* ushers us into the Holy of Holies where we can see the Lord high and lifted up. Through the corporate discipline of *guidance*, we can know in our own experience the cloud by day and the pillar of fire by night. *Celebration* offers the wonderful, hilarious, exuberant experience of walking and leaping and praising God.

These Disciplines of the spiritual life can be for us a means of receiving God's grace. They put us in a place where we can experience inner transformation as a gift. But there are pitfalls that can hinder our way. That is why I often speak of the Disciplines as the dangerous life of the Spirit. We must be diligent to avoid these pitfalls. Perhaps some advance warning will help. I would like to mention seven for you, although there are no doubt many more.

I.

The first pitfall is the temptation to make a law of the Disciplines. There is nothing that can choke the heart and soul out of walking with God like legalism. The rigid person is not the disciplined person. Rigidity is the most certain sign that the Disciplines have spoiled. The disciplined person is the person who can do what needs to be done when it needs to be done. The disciplined person is the person who can live appropriately in life. Jean-Pierre de Caussade put it so well: "The soul light as a feather, fluid as water, responds to the initiative of divine grace like a floating balloon."

Consider the story of Hans the tailor. Because of his reputation, an influential entrepreneur visiting the city ordered a tailor-made suit. But when he came to pick up this suit, the customer found that one sleeve twisted that way and the other this way; one shoulder bulged out and the other caved in. He pulled and struggled and finally, wrenched and contorted, he managed to make his body fit. As he returned home on the bus, another passenger noticed his odd appearance and asked if Hans the tailor had made the suit. Receiving an affirmative reply, the man remarked, "Amazing! I knew that Hans was a good tailor, but I had no idea he could make a suit fit so perfectly someone as deformed as you." Often that is just what we do in the church. We get some idea of what the Christian faith should look like: then we push and shove people into the most grotesque configurations until they fit wonderfully! That is death. It is a wooden legalism that destroys the soul.

Often my students who are working on the Spiritual Disciplines will keep a journal. When I read those journals I frequently must counsel the students to quit trying so hard to be religious. Let go a little bit! The Disciplines are a grace as well as a Discipline. There is an ease, a naturalness that flows as we walk with God. Some people are not ready for certain Disciplines and so should be kept from doing them. We should never encourage each other to embrace the Disciplines until there is an internal readiness.

The best way to keep the Spiritual Disciplines from becoming law is to show forth that inward spirit of freedom within us. As we model the life of righteousness, joy, and peace in the Holy Spirit, people will be attracted. They will be drawn into the most rigorous experiences of spiritual exercises without deadly legalism. Jesus was a man of spiritual discipline, but his life did not put people in bondage. It set them free. The same is true for Paul and Peter and all the saints. One cannot read *The Little Flowers of St. Francis* or Hudson Taylor's *Spiritual Secret* without being caught up in their sense of joy and freedom. We must remember that the Spiritual Disciplines are perceptions into life, not regulations for controlling life.

II.

The second pitfall is the failure to understand the social implications of the Disciplines. The Disciplines are not a set of pious exercises for the devout. They are a trumpet call to a freely gathered martyr people who know now the life and powers of the Kingdom of God. We are called to holy obedience in a sin wracked world. The Disciplines call us to wage peace in a world obsessed with war, to plead for justice in a world plagued by inequity, to stand with the poor and disinherited in a world where the neighbor is forgotten. We are to engage in the Lamb's War against sin in every area. This war is waged on all fronts at once—personal, social, institutional. Where have we gotten this foolish division of things spiritual and things secular? The life of disciplined obedience reaches into every sphere of human existence. We are called to attack evil wherever it is found, using all of the weapons available to us consistent with Ephesians 6. As James Naylor put it, Christ "puts spiritual weapons into our hearts and hands to make war with his enemies." We "conquer, not as the prince of this world . . . with whips and prisons, tortures and torments . . . But with the word of truth . . . returning love for hatred, wrestling with God against the enemy, with prayers and tears night and day, with fasting, mourning, and lamentation, in patience, in faithfulness, in truth, in love unfeigned, in long-suffering, and in all of the fruits of the Spirit, that if by any means we may overcome evil with good."

III.

The third pitfall is to view the Disciplines as virtuous in themselves. In and of themselves, the Disciplines have absolutely no virtue whatsoever. They will not make us righteous. They will not give us any brownie points with God. They do absolutely nothing except place us before God. This is the central truth many fail to see. They think the Disciplines can somehow make them righteous. So fasting, for instance, could become the key. It is this mistake that causes people to turn the Disciplines into a legalism. When we embrace a system, we have a hoop we can hold out for other people to jump through. But once we see that the Disciplines do not make us righteous, then we are free from all such systems. The function of the Disciplines is simply to place us before God. With that, they reach the end of their usefulness. The righteousness of the Kingdom of God is then a gift that comes to us.

IV.

A fourth and similar pitfall is to center on the Disciplines rather than on Christ. The Disciplines are for the purpose of realizing a greater good. One cannot play the game of soccer without rules, but the rules are not the game. I do not spend all day reading the rules of soccer and consider that a wonderful experience. The joy comes from playing the game. The rules of soccer are for the purpose of helping us realize the greater good, which is the experience of the game itself. The Spiritual Disciplines are for the purpose of realizing the greater good, which is the encounter with Christ himself. We must always focus our attention upon Christ rather than the Disciplines. It is not wrong to study and experiment with the Disciplines as long as we always remember that they are only leading us into the reality. The Disciplines are a means of grace to lead us into the grace itself.

V.

A fifth pitfall is the tendency to isolate or elevate one Discipline and exclude or neglect the others. When I received the sample printing of the cover for *Celebration of Discipline*, I died inside. I learned for the first time that the subtitle chosen by the publisher was "Paths to Spiritual Growth." Immediately I wrote a detailed letter in response, saying, essentially, "You missed the whole point." It is not "*paths*," as if each Discipline is a separate path which we can take without going down the others. It is "*path*." The Disciplines are a single reality. They are a seamless robe. It is like the fruit of the Spirit—not fruits but fruit. We cannot have love without having joy, peace, patience, kindness, goodness, faithfulness, gentleness, and self-control. These all describe a single reality, a single life. The same is true of the Spiritual Disciplines. Sometimes people will get intrigued, for example, with fasting, thinking this single Discipline will really lead them into God. Or, they will take up simplicity. They will go through all kinds of contortions to simplify their lives yet forget that this is only one part of a much larger picture. The Disciplines comprise an organic whole. For the life that is pleasing to God is not a series of religious duties. It is only one thing—to hear God's voice and to obey his word. The Disciplines are helpful only as they work together to enhance that life.

VI.

The sixth pitfall is to think that the twelve Disciplines that I have mentioned in this article and in *Celebration of Discipline* somehow exhaust the means of God's grace. This is a danger because it looks so neatly packaged—four inward Disciplines, four outward Disciplines, four corporate Disciplines. But Christ is greater than any attempt to describe his workings with his children. He cannot be confined to any system, no matter how worthy. As far as I know, there is no exhaustive list of the Christian Disciplines.

The Spiritual Disciplines are ways by which we place ourselves before God. Whatever ushers us into the Holy of Holies is proper and right for us to engage in. In my discussions, I have tried to concentrate on those Spiritual Disciplines that are universal. They are for all Christians at all times. But there are certainly other specific experiences and ways of coming before God that particular individuals will take up at particular times. We must let Christ be our ever-present Teacher to show us how we can learn better to walk with him.

There is a perennial temptation to confine Christ as we describe his workings with his children. We will read the *Spiritual Exercises* of St. Ignatius of Loyola or Jeremy Taylor's *Rule and Exercise of Holy Living*, and then we will turn them into another system that confines the work of the Spirit rather than sets us free. This temptation is strong when we enter into a wonderful experience of God's presence through particular circumstances: a certain kind of worship service, perhaps with an altar call or a particular hymn like "Just As I Am," a certain liturgy or setting, or a special posture such as kneeling. We think that somehow does it all, and in order to retain the experience, we repeat the circumstances. We take what was a living, vibrant reality and calcify and cement it. We destroy the very experience we seek.

There is a delightful little chorus that goes this way:

In a new and living way Jesus comes to us today.

The way he comes to us today will probably be different than the way he came to us yesterday; and tomorrow will be different from today. We must always be sensitive to these movements, so we do not confine the Holy Spirit. No description of the Spiritual Disciplines exhausts the way God works. He will probably teach us spiritual exercises that nobody has written anywhere.

VII.

The seventh pitfall is the most dangerous. It is the temptation to study the Disciplines without experiencing them. To discuss the

Disciplines in the abstract, to argue and debate their nature and validity—this we can do in relative safety. But to step out into experience threatens us at the core of our being. Nevertheless, there is no other way. We cannot learn the Spiritual Disciplines in the Western, abstract way. The knowledge comes through the experience. People will debate with me about meditation, for example, but there is only so far we can go in theoretical discussion. This is a field that is like science. We cannot avoid lab experiments. So I say, "Let's not talk about it. Let's do it. Then out of that experience we will reflect upon what happened." We do not debate whether it is possible to hear God; we try it and then see what happens.

Of course, people will say to me there is a danger of falling off the deep end. And that is a danger, but please remember there is also a danger of falling off the shallow end. When a person falls off the deep end, at least there is a chance of swimming. If you fall off the shallow end, you are going to break your neck.

In the famous book of Cervantes, *Don Quixote*, de la Mancha says, "It is one thing to praise discipline, and another to submit to it." May God give us the grace to jump in and get our feet wet in this adventurous life of the Spiritual Disciplines.

Excerpted from *Celebration of Discipline Study Guide* published in 1983 by HarperCollins.

Appendix F

Invitations to Speak,
Renovaré Conferences, Translations

(1) Invitations to Lecture on
Celebration of Discipline

What follows is a list of invitations Richard Foster received to speak on the role of the Disciplines as a means of grace in spiritual formation. As Richard was available to accept only one invitation per month, he chose which to accept through a process of corporate discernment.

Forty-one of the fifty states extended invitations. On nine different occasions, the esteemed Staley Distinguished Christian Scholar Lecture Program funded Richard's speaking engagements at various colleges and universities. Pastors from local churches across the United States and Canada and the leadership of twenty-four different Protestant denominations, Roman Catholics, and the Church of Latter-day Saints extended invitations for Richard Foster to teach their people about the spiritual Disciplines. Within a period of several years, Richard received invitations from fifty-seven colleges and universities, twenty-one seminaries, eight Christian parachurch organizations, several missionary organizations, and organizers of Christian bookseller conventions. Invitations came from Australia, China, Costa Rica, England, Germany, Hong Kong, Korea, and South Africa. The publisher was kept busy granting permission for the text to be translated for overseas markets.

1979 Invitations

Churches: Baptist, Church of the Savior, Friends, Mennonite
Colleges and Seminaries: Earlham School of Religion, Hesston College, Wheaton College
Christian Organizations: Holy Order of MANS, Quaker Hill

1980 Invitations

Churches: Free Methodist, Friends, Methodist, Reformed
Colleges and Seminaries: Bethel College, Fuller Seminary, Seattle Pacific University, Trinity College
Christian Organization: 700 Club
International: London, England

1985 Invitations

Churches: Assemblies of God, Authentic Life Church, Christian Reformed, Church of God, Evangelical Covenant, Evangelical Free, Friends, Disciples of Christ, Missionary Alliance, Nazarene, Presbyterian Church (USA), Southern Baptist Convention, United Methodist
Colleges and Seminaries: Columbia Seminary, Friends University, Princeton Seminary, Trevecca Nazarene College, Trinity Evangelical Divinity School
Christian Organization: Navigators

1986 Invitations

Churches: Assembly of God, Disciplined Order of Christ, Free Methodist, Episcopal, Evangelical Covenant, Mennonite, Pentecostal, United Church of Christ

Colleges and Seminaries: Asbury Theological Seminary, Azusa Pacific University, Columbia Seminary, Fresno Pacific College, John Brown University, North Park College, Regent College, Sterling College

Christian Organizations: Bear Trap, Group

International: England, Canada

*In 1986 Richard Foster sensed a leading from God to step away from his rigorous public ministry and devote himself more fully to silence. As it turned out, this period lasted eighteen months and resulted in the formation of Renovaré.

1988 Invitations

Churches: American Baptist, Baptist, Church of God, Church of the Brethren, Congregational, Disciples of Christ, Dutch Catholic, Episcopal, Evangelical Lutheran, Free Methodist, Friends, Missouri Baptist, Presbyterian Church (USA), Reformed Church, Southern Baptist, United Methodist Church, Wesleyan

Colleges and Seminaries: Asbury Theological Seminary, Bethel College, Biola University, Canadian Theological Seminary, Earlham School of Religion, Fuller Seminary, Maryville College, Messiah College, Moody Bible Institute, Pfeiffer United Methodist College, Regent College, Spring Arbor College, Taylor University, Warner Pacific College, Whitman College, Wichita State University, William Jewell College

Christian Organizations: Christian Resource Ministry, Eaton Rapids, Ecumenical Lecture Series, Evangelical

Christian Missionary Conference, Intervarsity, Lee Abbey Fellowship, Youth with a Mission

International: Church of England, Eaton Rapids (UK), United Church of Canada

1989 Invitations

Churches: American Baptist, Evangelical Lutheran Church of America, Friends, Latter-day Saints, Lutheran, Mennonite, Mennonite Brethren, North American Baptist, Pentecostal, Presbyterian Church (USA), Salvation Army, Seventh Day Adventist, Southern Baptist, South Carolina Baptist Convention, Swedish Baptist, United Church of Christ, United Methodist

Colleges and Seminaries: Columbia Theological Seminary, Earlham School of Religion, Fresno Pacific College, Goshen College, Northwestern University, Ontario Theological Seminary, Ottawa University, University of Lancaster

Christian Organizations: Camp Caroline (Canada), Young Life

International: Canada

1990 Invitations

Churches: Church of the Brethren, Episcopal, Evangelical Covenant, Evangelical Lutheran, Free Methodists, Friends, Mennonite, Missionary Church, Missouri Baptist Convention, Nazarene, North American Baptist, Pentecostal, Salvation Army, Southern Baptist, United Methodists, Vineyard

Colleges and Seminaries: Bethel College, Florida State University, Nazarene University, New Orleans Baptist Seminary, Seattle Pacific University, Southern Baptist Theological Seminary, Southern California College

Christian Organizations: Camp Caroline (Canada), Evangelical Christian Missionary Conference
International: Australia, Canada

1991 Invitations

Churches: American Baptist, Baptist, Church of the Brethren, Congregational, Episcopal, Evangelical Free, Evangelical Lutheran, Free Methodist, Jesuit, Methodist, Mennonite, Missouri Baptist Convention, Nazarene, Pentecostal, Reformed Church in America, Southern Baptist, Tennessee Baptist Convention, United Methodist, Wesleyan Evangelical Protestant Church

Colleges and Seminaries: Ashland Theological Seminary, Azusa Pacific University, Belmont University, Biola University, Central College of Iowa, Church of God Theological Seminary, East Baptist Theological Seminary, Evangelical Free Church of China, Fuller Seminary, Georgetown College, Hesston College, Indiana Wesleyan University, Messiah College, Northwestern Nazarene College, Regent University, South Carolina College, Southwest Baptist University, Stamford University, Trinity Evangelical Divinity School, Union College, Wheaton College

International: Costa Rica, Hong Kong, South Africa

1992 Invitations

Churches: American Baptist, Baptist, Christian Reformed, Episcopal, Free Methodists, Friends, Full Gospel, Latter-day Saints, Lutheran Missouri Synod, Mennonite, Nazarene, Pentecostal, Presbyterian Church (USA), Southern Baptist, United Church of Christ, United Methodist Church, Wesleyan

Colleges and Seminaries: Asbury Theological Seminary, Asian Theological Seminary, Earlham School of Religion,

Eastern College, Hesston College, Hollins College, Houghton College, Kings College, New College, Ontario Bible College, Seattle Pacific University, Southern Baptist Seminary, Southern California College, Southern Nazarene University, Southwestern Baptist, Sterling College, Trevecca Nazarene, University of Wisconsin, Wheaton College

Christian Organizations: Aqueduct Retreat Center

International: Canada, China, Germany, North Ireland, Philippines, Sweden

1993 Invitations

Churches: American Baptist, Baptist General Convention, Brethren in Christ, Mennonite, Mennonite Brethren, Nazarene, United Methodist.

Colleges and Seminaries: Baylor University, Duke Divinity School, Hesston College, Mennonite Brothers Seminary, Messiah College, Northern Baptist Seminary, Trevecca Nazarene College, Sioux Falls College

Christian Organization: Cedar Springs

International: Canada

1994 Invitations

Churches: Friends, Mennonite, Pentecostal, Presbyterian, Reformed Church in America, Southern Baptist, Church of God

Colleges and Seminaries: Anderson University, Bethel College and Seminary, Denver Seminary, Fuller Seminary, George Fox College, Schreiner College, Western Evangelical Seminary

Christian Organization: Young Life

International: Puerto Rico

(2) RENOVARÉ CONFERENCES AND RETREATS: 1989–2012

A total of thirty-six states sponsored Renovaré conferences and
retreats.

    a. Regional, National, International Conferences (total
attendance 57,000)

1989	Kansas
1991	Kansas, California
1992	Kansas, California (2)
1993	California, Michigan, Massachusetts, Minnesota, Missouri
1994	Colorado, Texas, Oregon (2), Indiana, Washington
1995	Massachusetts, California, North Carolina, South Carolina, Washington, Texas
1996	Texas, Oklahoma, Louisiana, Kentucky, Maryland, Michigan, California (2)
1997	Texas, Oregon, New York, Colorado, Tennessee, Ohio, Virginia, Kentucky
1998	Texas, North Carolina, California, Montana, Iowa, Alabama, Indiana
1999	Texas (3), Kentucky, Ohio, Indiana, Washington, Illinois
2000	Oklahoma, Arizona, Pennsylvania, Texas, Washington, Tennessee, California, North Carolina
2001	California, North Carolina, Kansas, Colorado, Minnesota, Texas
2002	California (3), Arizona, Maryland, Ohio, Georgia
2003	Florida, California, Pennsylvania, Virginia, Colorado, Louisiana
2004	California, Washington, North Carolina, Minnesota, Alabama, Ohio, Kentucky

2005   California (2), Florida, Texas, Colorado,
        Florida, Maine
2006   Washington, Ohio, Virginia, Texas, West
        Virginia
2007   Oklahoma (2), Florida, Pennsylvania,
        California (2), Indiana
2008   Texas, North Carolina, Nebraska, Georgia,
        New Brunswick, Canada

b. Seminars on Renovaré Covenant Groups (total
    attendance 1,000)
1989   Kansas
1990   Kansas (2), California (2)
1991   California (2)
1997   Texas

c. Renovaré Retreats (total attendance 2,100)
1992   Colorado
1993   Colorado (3), Missouri
1994   Colorado (2), Missouri
1995   Kansas
1997   Texas
2001   Maryland
2004   Colorado
2006   Colorado
2008   Colorado
2010   California

d. Renovaré Local Conferences (total attendance
    2,600)
1995   Montana, Kansas
1996   Oregon, Idaho, Missouri, California, Colorado
1997   Indiana, Georgia
1999   Vancouver, Canada
2001   Alabama, Ohio, Washington, Florida, Kansas
2003   Illinois, Michigan, California, Alabama,
        Florida, Maryland
2004   Colorado, Michigan, Maryland, Kansas

2005	New Hampshire, California
2006	Minnesota
2007	Oklahoma, Pennsylvania, North Carolina
2008	New York, Arkansas

e. Renovaré Special Events (total attendance 1,100)

2003	Texas
2007	California

f. Renovaré Britain & Ireland Conferences (total attendance unknown)

2003	Altrincham, England
2004	Prestwick, Scotland
2006	London, Brighton, Winchester events

g. Renovaré VIM (Vision, Intention, Means) Conferences (attendance 650)

2003	Kentucky
2004	Georgia, California

h. Renovaré Africa Conferences (total attendance unknown)

2004	Nairobi, Kenya
2007	Various events

i. Renovaré Korea Conferences (total attendance unknown)

2002	Los Angeles, California
2003	Los Angeles, California
2004	Virginia, Maryland
2005	Virginia
2007	Seoul, South Korea
2008	Toronto, Canada

j. Renovaré Essentials Conferences (total attendance unknown)

2009	North Carolina, California, Colorado, Texas, Maryland
2010	California, Arizona, Texas, South Dakota
2011	Colorado, Oklahoma, Michigan, Pennsylvania
2012	Texas (2), Pennsylvania

(3) *Celebration of Discipline* Translations (33 Languages)

Afrikaans, Albanian, Amharic, Arabic, Burmese, Chinese (traditional), Chinese (simplified), Croatian, Czech, Dutch, French, German, Hebrew, Indonesian, Italian, Japanese, Korean, Lithuanian, Macedonian, Mongolian, Persian, Polish, Portuguese, Romanian, Russian, Serbian, Spanish, Swedish, Turkish, Vietnamese.

Adding the three pending contracts for Bulgarian, Urdu, and Tajik, the total number of translations is 33.

The current translations of *Celebration of Discipline*.

Dallas Willard article (abridged):

"Defense of Visualization Against Certain Theological Objections"

If you are at all active in the larger Christian community, you are no doubt aware of the divisiveness that has arisen around the topic of imagery, visualization, imagination, and even psychology as a whole. I do not need to defend psychology, but there are many who are still afraid of visualization [in the practice of contemplation] and have shied away from its use. Imagery prayer is needed because of its ability to open pathways in the heart that are closed to the presence of Christ under the more commonly used ministries of the church.

If we could "just tell" people from the pulpit to confess Christ and to pray, if their behavior were changed by that alone, then there would, of course, be no further problem. If all people were able to respond to what they hear from the pulpit and put that into practice in their lives, and if they then had a valid, scriptural concept of God as Helper, Comforter, Deliverer and Guide—a God to be worshipped and adored—then we would have no need for any other methods. But the message from the pulpit often does not have this effect. To many individuals, it even brings fruitless condemnation and paralysis, rather than conviction and change, because they have locked away within them dreadful "images" of God and horrible experiences with people who "taught" them of God. For them, something beyond the usual church service is needed. . . .

But various contemporary Christian writers have bitterly attacked such a practice. It would serve no purpose to mention them by name here, but we do want to reply to a number of objections they raise. . . . In general, the complaint is that such techniques as we have described are contrary to Scripture and are "merely human" or even involve cooperation with Satan or evil spirits. We will break this down into separate points after a few preliminary comments.

First of all, we are called, as were Jesus' first disciples, to do the works he did: "Verily, verily, I say unto you, he that believeth on me, the works that I do shall he do also . . ." (John 14:12).

Secondly, what was finished at the cross was necessary for the forgiveness of our sins, not the process of growth in grace, the transformation of our sin-scarred souls into conformity to Christ. God sends his Word of the gospel into our souls to bring the new life of faith; and we can, like Paul, be confident "that he which hath begun a good work in you will perform it until the day of Jesus Christ" (Phil. 1:6), when that now clearly unfinished work will be completed.

Thirdly, in this ongoing and unfinished work of Christ in us, we have an indispensable role. Because of the ultimately assured cosmic triumph of Christ, we are exhorted now to be bold and to "work out your own salvation with fear and trembling. For it is God which worketh in you both to will and to do of his good pleasure" (Phil. 2:12–13). Therefore, we are commanded to "put on therefore, as the elect of God, holy and beloved, bowels (those are inward) of mercies, kindness, humbleness of mind, meekness, longsuffering," (etc., etc., Col. 3:12–23), even though there is no question of our doing it without God's help. It will not simply be done for us.

Fourthly, the . . . great Ephesians passage (4:12ff) on the ministry of the church for the perfecting or "completing" of the saints makes it clear that those in leadership positions are to work with God to accomplish the inner transformation of those who have accepted Christ as their Savior.

This is a fact. The only questions concern the required or admissible means for carrying out the charge. But now the objections:

VISUALIZATION IS AN OCCULT PRACTICE.

We acknowledge that visualization can be misused and that it has been misused by various occult groups throughout the ages. The objection is that visualization can *only* be occult and hence a work of Satan. But we have already established that imagery and visualization are present throughout human life. Is everyone, then, involved in the occult just because they have imagery and visualize things? Of course not! As our friend Richard Foster writes in his marvelous book, *Celebration of Discipline,* "Some have objected to using the imagination out of concern that it is untrustworthy and could even be used by the Evil One. There is good reason for concern, for the imagination, like all our faculties, has participated in the Fall. But just as we can believe that God can take our reason (fallen as it is) and sanctify it and use it for his good purposes, so we believe he can sanctify the imagination and use it for his good purposes. Of course, the imagination can be distorted by Satan, but then so can all our faculties. God created us with an imagination, and as Lord of his creation, he can and does redeem it and use it for the work of the Kingdom of God. . . . To believe that God can sanctify and utilize the imagination is simply to take seriously the Christian idea of incarnation. God so accommodates, so enfleshes himself into our world, that he uses the images we know and understand to teach us about the unseen world of which we know so little and which we find so difficult to understand."[222]

Then it is not *visualization* that is an occult practice but a certain way of using it. The use of visualization in the occult is one where the user's faith is in demonic powers or in magical powers attributed to imagery itself. Above all, it is a use in which the users wish merely to get what they want and are willing to try to manipulate God or anything else to that end. We examine its use: What is its purpose? What is its content? Who does it honor? Whose blessing does it seek? This examination should be applied to the practice of visualization, inner healing, therapy, and to the uses of images, thoughts, words, etc.

VISUALIZATION IS NOT TAUGHT IN THE SCRIPTURES.

Here we come upon one of those claims of the critic that is simply untrue. Visualization is a way of thinking about anything upon which we wish to concentrate with great intensity. The Apostle Paul exhorts the Philippian believers: "Whatever is true, whatever is honorable, whatever is right, whatever is pure, whatever is lovely, whatever is of good report, if there is any excellence and if anything worthy of praise, let your mind dwell on these things" (4:8 NASV). Our minds dwell on things mainly by visualizing them, so far as may be possible. To command someone to mentally concentrate upon a certain thing is, because of the nature of the mind, to command them to use their powers of imagery and visualization, just as to command someone to cross the street is to command them to move parts of their body to accomplish the crossing, though no movements of bodily parts are mentioned.

This same truth comes into play with other scriptural passages, such as Hebrews 3:1: "Therefore, holy brethren, partakers of a heavenly calling, consider Jesus, the apostle and High Priest of our confession" (NASV). And in Hebrews 12:2, a term, *aphorontes*, is used, which could quite properly be translated as "visualizing:" "Fixing our eyes on <visualizing> Jesus, the author and perfecter of faith" (Colossians 3:2). Ironically, as we shall see below, one of the very verses that critics have cited as contrary to visualization commands those who have received resurrection life to "set your mind on the things above, not on the things that are on the earth." Jesus is, of course, the one we focus on to do this, and he himself is described in Hebrews 1:3 as the exact representation or "image" of God.

This present objection is, then, simply false. But even if visualization were not commanded in the Scripture, that would not by itself mean it is wrong. For many things that are good and right are not taught in the Scriptures. For instance, Sunday schools, Bible colleges, mission boards, printing presses, paper, bound books, TV, motion pictures, tape recordings are non-scriptural means for making known the gospel. I fully agree with David Seamands' statement: "The real question is not whether a practice appears in the Bible in the specific form or language we use today. Rather, the question is whether it is contradictory to or consistent with principles stated in Scripture."[223]

It is important, however, to understand that visualization as an activity of the human mind is taught, is *commanded*, in the Scriptures. Nevertheless, some have objected that the use of visualization in [ministries such as] inner healing is contrary to Scripture, not just because it is visualization but because it attempts to deal with the past, which they say Scripture instructs us to disregard altogether.

The first thing to be said here is that inner healing is not primarily a matter of dealing with the past but with the present. Memories are not in the past but in the present. What they are of or about is in the past. Inner healing through imagery and prayer is wholly directed toward changing the present and the future condition of the individual's heart, mind, and soul. Once again, we must keep in mind that inner healing, the restoration of the soul, is a major part of God's redemptive work in us as portrayed in the Old and New Testaments. The Old Testament passage, which Jesus took for his own job description as Messiah, charged him with, among other things, the healing of the broken hearted, delivering the captives, comforting those who mourn, giving beauty for ashes, the oil of joy for mourning, and the garment of praise for the spirit of heaviness (Isaiah 61:13; Luke 4:17–19). And we are called, as were his first disciples, to do the works he did: "Verily, verily, I say unto you, he that believeth on me, the works that I do shall he do also . . ." (John 14:12).

So, there is no question about the legitimacy of inner healing from the scriptural point of view. We are under command to see to it that it is done. Anything less is simply a failure to serve others in love. "Outer healing" alone would but "make clean the outside of the cup and of the platter, but within they are full of extortion and excess" (Matthew 23:25).

Secondly, what was *finished* at the cross was necessary for the forgiveness of our sins, not the process of growth in grace, the transformation of our sin-scarred souls into conformity to Christ. God sends his Word of the gospel into our souls to bring the new life of faith; and we can, like Paul, be confident "that he which hath begun a good work in you will perform it until the day of Jesus Christ" (Philippians 1:6), when that now clearly *unfinished* work will be completed.

Thirdly, in this ongoing and *unfinished work of Christ in us*, we have an indispensable role. Because of the ultimately assured cosmic triumph of Christ, we are exhorted now to be bold and to "work out your own salvation with fear and trembling. For it is God which worketh in you both to will and to do of his good pleasure" (Philippians 2:12–13). Therefore, we are commanded to "put on therefore, as the elect of God, holy and beloved, bowels (those are inward) of mercies, kindness, humbleness of mind, meekness, longsuffering," (etc., etc., Colossians 3:12–23), even though there is no question of our doing it without God's help. It will not simply be done *for* us.

Fourthly, the helping ministries of Christians to Christians obviously involve aiding individuals who have saving faith in

Christ to work out their own salvation as just indicated. Thus, the great Ephesians passage (4:12ff) on the ministry of the church for the perfecting or "completing" of the saints makes it clear that those in leadership positions are to work with God to accomplish the inner transformation of those who have accepted Christ as their Savior.

We conclude by reiterating that the present and future is our concern in visualization with (meditation or) prayer and that present misconceptions of the past are changed by prayerful, Spirit-enabled reconsiderations of traumatic past events and relationships in the light of the gospel. No scriptural teaching is contrary to this practice.

Summary of Willard's perspective on the use of imagination in contemplation and meditation:

- **Imagery is a natural human ability that is present in every human mind.** Images occur. Period. They occur constantly, in every mind. No mind—no personality—fails to be influenced by them. They *are*, they have their effects, whether we wish it or not.
- **There is nothing inherently evil or wrong about images**. Images may be expressions of evil and influence the individual toward evil or harm, but they may equally serve as expressions of good and influence the individual toward good and benefit.
- **As in every area of human action, images are partially under the direction of our will and partially not.** The meaning of finitude is limitation, not inability. We find the limits of our ability and, within them, are response*able*. We are responsible under God to act for his glory within our limitations, always looking to him in faith to determine the outcome.
- **Imagery is widely recognized as a dimension of conscious experience through which the dynamics of the self can be understood and affected.** [224]

Reverend Doctor Derek Oppenshaw,
Supernumerary Minister,
Methodist Church of Southern Africa article:

"Celebration of Discipline"

How many Christ followers have struggled with the practice of a quiet or devotional time somewhere in their spiritual walk? Being discouraged, feeling unworthy when reading the Bible and praying, the primary items on a disciple's "must do" list, becomes a burden instead of the blessing it was intended to be? Guilt floods the soul, and legalism infiltrates discipleship! "Must do" is heavy! How many Christ followers have felt this way?

Quiet time—devotional time, labelled as essential, central to discipleship, where available resources in the '60s through to early '80s focused primarily on Bible reading and prayer. Authors mainly used the Psalmist David or Jesus as template—hence, biblical devotional time is early in the morning.[225] In the modern world, many find early morning difficult and attempts at other daily fixed times also did not work out. This created more of the unfortunate feelings described above. A failure at setting and religiously maintaining one's quiet time even has a way of throwing doubt on one's salvation. Or so it felt.

In such a world, seemingly void of readily available resources covering a wider spectrum of Spiritual Disciplines, I perchance lifted *Celebration* (1978) off a dusty bookshelf. Curiously running a finger down the table of contents, a chapter heading drew my attention. A simple heading that was to ignite a continual paradigm shift: *"The Spiritual Disciplines: Door to Liberation."* Liberation! Eagerly devouring Foster's work, admittedly far too quickly, a new perspective, understanding, and interest in Spiritual Disciplines emerged. This "new" has remained ever since. Currently, my personal library collection proudly exhibits the 2005 version of Foster's work.

There is always something fresh in the practice of Spiritual Disciplines when approached through the lens of *liberation* as opposed to—*must do*! Indeed, "dull drudgery" can be replaced by joy as keynote.[226] Yes, these practices are essential, remain central, and always will be. But now, no longer something to do but rather experienced. Indeed, a *person* to be experienced.

Around the same time of acquiring *Celebration*, I discovered Wesley's deemed perspective regarding devotionals, which is best described by Harper (1998:10): "God does not call you to have a devotional time; God calls you to live a devotional life." This discovery helped integrate Spiritual Disciplines and life. No longer were Spiritual Disciplines something that life did, rather the Disciplines *breathed life*. Liberation!

A stumbling block in contemporary Christianity is the term, "discipline" and its perceived bias of legalism. Personally, I have wrestled with this myself and through much reading and thought arrived at describing "discipline" as "placing oneself in a position where God's Spirit can work with one the best, the most." This theological approach, I believe, is supported by Foster in his 1983 work: *Study Guide for Celebration of Discipline*, in writing that "our only work—is to place ourselves in the way of Christ and invite him to work in our lives individually and corporately." I found this study guide supplement to *Celebration* exceptionally helpful.

Furthermore, not only did *Celebration* present a much wider spectrum of Spiritual Disciplines than Christ followers may initially have envisaged but it also addressed how certain practices that were not identified as a specific Discipline integrated into other Disciplines. A good example of this is *silence*, which is not presented as a primary named Discipline but an associated or sub-discipline of the twelve identified. The discovery of the gamut, associations, and depth of the Disciplines was both enlightening and challenging. Enlightening, not only epistemologically but that it created a curiosity as to early Wesleyan/Methodist spiritual practices. Challenging to reverently explore and creatively experience the different practices to experience the life they may breathe into my every day. Through examining the practices theologically and exercising them, it was enlightening to discover that Spiritual Disciplines are not "fluffy spiritual" but involve body, mind, and spirit—indeed, the whole of one's being.

After encountering a broader perspective of the Disciplines through *Celebration*, I have sought other works on the subject. I found working through the writings of John Wesley, Dallas Willard, John Ortberg, and Joyce Rupp, to mention a few, very enriching. I often remind Methodists that we are not of the reformed tradition but emerged out of the Anglican tradition, which, in turn, is of Roman Catholic origin. My favorite saying: "Our mother is Anglican, and our grandmother is Roman Catholic!" Hence, I have also gained much through exploring and experiencing the ways of practicing Spiritual Disciplines through these traditions.

Although some of the Disciplines are seen as primary, daily practices, yet by intentionally focusing on a different Discipline each week led me to appreciate the *what, why, how* and *where* of every practice's ministry into my life. This also gives opportunity for diverse experiences of God's presence. Once again—liberation!

There appears to be a common current of apathy toward the practice of fasting. This I found most challenging and even fascinating in a sense. Many explanations have been given for not following this Discipline, ranging from its perceived, expected length, its constitution, to medical reasons. The most prevalent being diabetes. To this end, it was encouraging to engage with vegetarians and vegans—some of whom fast as a principle of health. These discussions have helped to present different approaches to fasting from both a health and spiritual perspective. Particularly helpful in this regard are the Daniel fasts,[227] the various partial fasts, and the Wesley fast.[228] These approaches to fasting have assisted in removing the burden of the classic phrase: "What would Jesus do" to Foster's word: "Liberation!" Thus, the *why* of the fast outweighs the duration and constitution thereof. In essence, gradually growing in the practice of fasting rather than undertaking a painful, virgin, forty-day experience.

Another Discipline that morphed over time in my experience was *study*—particularly when focusing on Scripture. The inner struggle and tensions between knowledge, application, and the desire for concrete evidence of Christlikeness within was tiresome, even discouraging. With *Celebration* as starting point, augmented by reading various respected authors on Bible study, and working through Wesley's perspective of "living a devotional life"—it dawned on me. Hence, a confession!

I have stopped reading the Bible! Now, I let the Bible read me. Letting Scripture "read me" within my own context creates a thirst within to gain more understanding of the original cultures, contexts, and purpose of the text. It also helps in finding myself within the biblical writing—indeed, a humbling experience.

In a recent ecumenical study on "The state of the clergy in South Africa," focusing on spiritual disciplines, *Celebration* was used as foundational source. The project leader's response when asked of this choice, was that "*[Celebration]* was and still is regarded as the contemporary seminal work on the topic." As the Methodist leader on this project, I was able to ascertain that, in general, South African Methodists are not overly familiar with Foster's work. This is especially so within previously disadvantaged communities. However, many had encountered the Disciplines Foster addresses in *Celebration* through diverse means. People who had used Foster's work found it to be "helpful." The ample examples of *what* constitutes each Discipline and creative and diverse examples of *how* to exercise them is most appreciated. However, a few felt that not enough clarity of the *why* behind each of the Disciplines is discussed—despite Foster suggesting possible outcomes and benefits. My observation is that it seems that Foster covers more of the *why* of specific Disciplines in his subsequent works and that *Celebration* was the launch pad. In this regard, I found Foster's study guide (1983) more helpful.

When encouraging Methodists to follow Foster's works,[229] as he developed them over time, I remind them of the Methodist-Quaker conversations that influenced the development of early Methodism. It is noteworthy that these conversations have, in some quarters, continued to this day.[230]

My journey as a Wesleyan, within the group called Methodist, growing in the understanding, practice, and ministry of Spiritual Disciplines, led me to an interpretation of Spiritual Disciplines—which I necessarily do not expect others to agree with:

Spiritual Disciplines are age-old means of "drawing near to God" (Wesley, 1987:85:825) "in the pursuit of spiritual formation, the pursuit of Christlikeness" (Tracy, 2013:1), thereby growing in holiness (Watson, 2009:97). The desired outcome to which one aspires is described as "perfect love" (Maddox, 1994:180), or entire sanctification or Christian perfection (Wesley, 1872:11:387), the axis around which Wesleyan spirituality revolves (Forster, 2001:1).

The opening question of this article asked: "How many Christ followers . . . ?" Well, this is one such Christ follower who would, I believe, never have reached such a description of Spiritual Disciplines or led spiritual retreats if it had not been for the perchance lifting of *Celebration of Discipline* off the bookshelf.

Perchance? Or—

BIBLIOGRAPHY

Forster, D., 2001, *An Introduction to Wesleyan Spirituality*, Methodist Publishing House, Cape Town, SA.

Foster, R., 2005, *Celebration of Discipline*, Hodder & Stoughton Ltd, London.

Harper, S., 1998, *Devotional Life in the Wesleyan Tradition: A Workbook*, Upper Room, Nashville, Tenn.

Maddox, R.L., 1994, *Responsible Grace: John Wesley's Practical Theology*, Kingswood Books, Nashville, Tenn.

Tracy, W.D., 2013, "Embrace Your Heritage: Spiritual Formation in the Wesleyan Tradition," *Adult Faith Connections Leader's Guide*, DJF 2013–14. The Foundry Publishing. Kansas City, MO.

Watson, K.M., 2009, *A Blueprint for Discipleship: Wesley's General Rules as a Guide for Christian Living*, Discipleship Resources, Nashville, TN.

Wesley, J., 1872, *The Works of John Wesley*, vol. 5, Wesleyan Methodist Bookroom, London, England.

Wesley, J., 1987, *Sermons on Several Occasions*, Moorley's Print & Publishing, Ilkeston, UK.

Jonathan Bailey essay:

"The Relationship Between Spiritual Discipline and Virtue"

When Richard Foster sat down to write *Celebration of Discipline*, I wasn't even born yet. It wouldn't be until twenty-three years after my birth that I picked up a copy of *Celebration* and read these words:

> Perhaps somewhere in the subterranean chambers of your life you have heard the call to deeper, fuller living. You have become weary of frothy experiences and shallow teaching. Every now and then you have caught glimpses, hints of something more than you have known. Inwardly you long to launch out into the deep.

After reading these lines, I was launched. Richard's words articulated the longing of my heart. For most of my Christian life, I had read books that taught me *why*, books that taught me *what*. But when I picked up *Celebration*, I finally found a book that taught me *how*. How to get in on the *with-God* life, how to practically follow Jesus, and how to experience genuine transformation by training with the Spiritual Disciplines.

I remember resting in a comfortable chair, practicing the discipline of silence, which actually felt more like wrestling than resting. To chase away distraction, I used a focal word, *love*, which was a gentle way of returning my thoughts to God. I had done this many times before, but on this occasion, something simple and sublime happened. When I said the word, *love*, it was like a single, solitary raindrop struck the interior of my heart, and a great ripple of divine love raced across my chest. The only way I can describe it to you now is to say that it felt like the purest and most potent form of joy, something infinite and indestructible.

It lasted seconds and faded. But what remained (I slowly discovered) was a fresh degree of freedom from one of my most stubborn vices: gluttony. This gift of freedom—the virtue of temperance—enabled an easy obedience, the kind that didn't feel like I was obeying. It didn't feel like I was acquiescing to a foreign will. It felt like I was responding to the natural surging of my own, which, wonder of wonders, I was. This was the kind of transformation Richard described in *Celebration*:

> A farmer is helpless to grow grain; all he can do is provide the right conditions for the growing of grain. He cultivates the ground, he plants the seed, he waters the plants, and then the natural forces of the earth take over and up comes the grain. . . .This is the way it is with the Spiritual Disciplines—they are a way of sowing to the Spirit. . . . By themselves the Spiritual Disciplines can do nothing; they can only get us to the place where something can be done.

Practicing the discipline of silence didn't give me virtue; it put me in a position to receive it. My role is to simply train with Jesus, to sow seeds, to give my life to the practice of the Disciplines. Learning this one truth has made all the difference.

The more I put it into practice, the more buds begin to bloom: "first the blade, then the ear, then the full grain" (Mk 4:28).

Most books are out of print after a couple of years but not *Celebration*. It's a perennial seller, an evergreen in Christian spirituality. Why? Because it moves us beyond nominal Christianity toward something essential and enduring. It's a rare achievement, to continue impacting readers decades after publication. But such is the case. In *Celebration*, we find a timeless expression of the call to discipleship, the call to follow Jesus, to slip into the easy yoke, and train. I will always be grateful for *Celebration of Discipline*. It opened me up to a whole new world of transformation. It gave me a fresh vision for *training* instead of *trying*. It shifted the whole trajectory of my life.

Endnotes

1 The Apostle Paul writes, "We have this treasure in earthen vessels." The treasure he notes is "the glory of God in the face of Jesus Christ." The earthen vessel is the human body and the various forms and liturgies we have for enshrouding the treasure (2 Corinthians 4:1–7).

2 "Books of the Century" (*Christianity Today*, April 24, 2000), https://www.christianitytoday.com/ct/2000/april24/5.92.html.

3 See "Spiritual Formation." *Wikipedia* (updated March 20, 2021), https://en.wikipedia.org/wiki/Spiritual_formation.

4 The Inward Disciplines of Meditation, Prayer, Fasting, and Study; the Outward Disciplines of Simplicity, Solitude, Submission, and Service; the Corporate Disciplines of Confession, Worship, Guidance, and Celebration.

5 Richard J. Foster, *Celebration of Discipline: the Path to Spiritual Growth* (Harper & Row, 1978), p. 1.

6 Priscilla Coit Murphy, *What a Book Can Do*, (University of Massaschusetts, 2005), p. 2.

7 Michael Maudlin, publisher at HarperCollins, email comment dated 12/4/2019.

8 Quoted by Gerald L. Sittser, *Water from a Deep Well*, (InterVarsity Press, 2007), p. 10.

9   C.S. Lewis, introduction to *St. Athanasius: On the Incarnation* (Crestwood, N.Y.: St. Vladimir's Seminary Press, 1993), p. 5, quoted by Gerald Sittser, *Water from a Deep Well*, p. 20.

10 Elton Trueblood, *The Incendiary Fellowship* (Harper & Row, 1967), pp. 63, 67.

11 Edward England, *The Unfading Vision: The Adventure of Books* (Media Associates International, 1982, 1999), p. 103.

12 England, p. 105.

13 "An Interview with Richard Foster," *Evangelical Friend*, October, 1981, pp. 6 &7.

14 *Christian Woman*, 1983.

15 *Voice of the Southwest*, Gallup, NM, Feb. 9, 1986.

16 Tommy Tyson, evangelist. Submitted to honor the 10th anniversary of the publication of *Celebration of Discipline*.

17 Chris McFadden, submitted to honor the 40th anniversary of the publication of *Celebration of Discipline*.

18 Phyllis Tickle, *God-Talk in America* (Crossroad Publishing Company, 1997), p. 9, 17.

19 Phyllis A. Tickle, *Re-Discovering the Sacred: Spirituality in America* (Crossroad, 1995),pp. 39, 42–43, 47.

20 Curt Thompson, M.D., *Anatomy of the Soul: Surprising connections between neuroscience and spiritual practices that can transform your life and relationships* (Tyndale Momentum, 2010), p. 15.

21 Gerald L. Sittser, *Water from a Deep Well: Christian Spirituality from Early Martyrs to Modern Missionaries* (IVP, 2007), p. 17.

22 Phyllis A. Tickle, *God-Talk in America* (Crossroads Publishing Company, 1997), p. 113.

23 Eugene Peterson, author of *Reversed Thunder* and *A Long Obedience in the Same Direction*. Submitted to honor the 10th anniversary of the publication of *Celebration of Discipline*.

24 "30 Years of Wisdom, Faith, and Healing from HarperOne" (Fall 2007) quoting Brian McLaren, author of *A New Kind of Christian*.

25 Richard J. Foster, *Celebration of Discipline: The Path to Spiritual Growth* (Harper One, Harper Collins, 2018 Special Anniversary edition), p. ix.

26 "Books of the Century," Christianity Today, April 24, 2000 issue.

27 George Marsden, *C.S. Lewis's Mere Christianity: A Biography* (Princeton University Press, 2016), pp. 1–2.

28 Matthew 6:33; C.S. Lewis, "First and Second Things," *God in the Dock* (Grand Rapids, MI: William Be. Eerdmans Publishing Company 1970), pp. 278–280.

29 Jodie Muller. Submitted to honor the 40th anniversary of the publication of *Celebration of Discipline* (12/2/2018).

30 Todd Hunter, from a Zoom video interview, September 25, 2020.

31 Phyllis Tickle, *Emergence Christianity: What It is, Where It Is Going, and Why It Matters* (Baker Books, 2012), p. 24.

32 Phyllis Tickle, *Emergence Christianity*, pp. 17–21.

33 Tickle, *Emergence Christianity*, p. 24.

34 Life Magazine Special Issue, "The 1960s: The Decade When Everything Changed," published July 26, 2016.

35 Nick Page, *A Nearly Infallible History of Christianity* (Hodder & Stoughton, 2013), p. 418.

36 "The 1950s—Powerful Years for Religion," Carol Tucker (USC News, June 16, 1997).

37 George Gallup Jr., "Is America's Faith for Real?" *Alumni/ae News*, Princeton Theological Seminary (Fall/Winter 1982):16.

38 *The Unchurched American* (Princeton: Princeton Religious Research Center, 1978), p. 8.

39 Michael L. Birkel, *Silence and Witness: the Quaker Tradition* (Orbis Books, Maryknoll, New York, 2004), pp. 17–18.

40 Birkel, pp. 56–57.

41 Thomas Cahill, "The Hinges of History," *How the Irish Saved Civilization* (Doubleday, 1995).

42 C. Peter Wagner, Professor of Church Growth, Fuller Seminary School of World Mission.

43 Laura Ingalls Wilder, *The Long Winter: Little House on the Prairie, Book 6* (HarperCollins, 1940).

44 Parker Palmer, *A Hidden Holiness: The Journey Toward an Undivided Life* (Jossey-Bass, 2004), p. 1.

45 Attributed to Martin Luther.

46 Richard Foster, Unpublished *Memoir*, ch. 1.

47 Ibid.

48 Psalm 46:10.

49 Richard Foster, Unpublished *Memoir*, ch. 1.

50 Ibid.

51 Foster's D.Th.P. dissertation sought to construct a theology of non-violent direct action for social change (*Quaker Concern in Race Relations: Then and Now*).

52 Richard Foster, "Seeking and Finding," (*Christian Century*, December 24–31, 1997), p. 12 & 13.

53 "Interview with Richard Foster," Grace Christus, *Epiphany* Magazine, Fall 1981, p. 68).

54 Ibid, Grace Christus, p. 68.

55 C.S. Lewis cited by Edward England, *The Unfading Vision: The Adventure of Books* (Media Associates International, 1982), p. 5.

56 The Leach family did not get John's last name.

57 Submitted by LaNeal Leach Miller, January 14, 2022.

58 Works-righteousness—the attempt to earn salvation by our actions.

59 Florence Lawson, *Palladium-Item* Religion Writer, December 16, 1979.

60 "An Interview with Richard Foster," *Evangelical Friend*, October 1981, p. 7.

61 Roy M. Carlisle, "Paradigmatic Shifts in Christian Publishing: An Editorial Perspective the Last Fifty Years (1969–2019)", p. 5.

62 Email from Tony Collins dated April 24, 2020.

63 Email from Carolyn Armitage, former Publishing Director, Hodder & Stoughton Religious Books, May 1, 2020.

64 Dallas Willard, submitted to honor the 10th anniversary of the publication of *Celebration of Discipline*.

65 "An Interview with Richard Foster," *Evangelical Friend*, October 1981, p. 9.

66 Review written by the Fuller Seminary Bookstore, January 1989.

67 Mark O. Hatfield, submitted to honor the 10th anniversary of the publication of *Celebration of Discipline*. 90 Macrina Wiederkehr, O.B.S., author of *A Tree Full of Angels*). Submitted to honor the 10th anniversary of the publication of *Celebration of Discipline*.

68 Lewis S. Smedes, author of *Caring & Commitment* and *Forgive & Forget*. Submitted to honor the 10th anniversary of the publication of *Celebration of Discipline*.

69 Madeleine L'Engle, author of *A Wrinkle in Time* and *The Crosswicks Journals*. Submitted to honor the 10th anniversary of the publication of *Celebration of Discipline*.

70 Richard J. Foster, *Celebration of Discipline: The Path to Spiritual Growth Special Anniversary Edition* (HarperOne, 2018), p. 206.

71 *Renewal*, June 1989.

72 Leanne Van Dyk, Lee Abbey *Rapport*, July/August.

73 Anna Bolch is with Hope Writers, an online writing community. From an email dated January 26, 2021.

74 Jamie Buckingham, submitted to honor the 40th anniversary of the publication of *Celebration of Discipline*.

75 Helen Washington, submitted to honor the 40th anniversary of the publication of *Celebration of Discipline*.

76 Wayne Kofink (Mennonite Pastor), submitted to honor the 40th anniversary of the publication of *Celebration of Discipline*.

77 Michael S. Rogers, submitted to honor the 40th anniversary of the publication of *Celebration of Discipline*.

78 Judith Lechman, author of *Yielding to Courage* and *The Spirituality of Gentleness*. Submitted to honor the 40th anniversary of the publication of *Celebration of Discipline*, reflecting on the meaning of the book in her life and practice of spirituality.

79 Barbara Bliss. Submitted to honor the 40th anniversary of the publication of *Celebration of Discipline* (12/2/2018).

80 Wendy Palmer, submitted to honor the 40th anniversary of the publication of *Celebration of Discipline*.

81 Chris Simpson, submitted to honor the 40th anniversary of the publication of *Celebration of Discipline*.

82 Connie Pittman, submitted to honor the 40th anniversary of the publication of *Celebration of Discipline*.

83 David L. McKenna, former President, Asbury Theological Seminary. Submitted to honor the 10th anniversary of the publication of *Celebration of Discipline*.

84 Luci Shaw, author of *Listen to the Green*. Submitted to honor the 10th anniversary of the publication of *Celebration of Discipline*.

85 Beth Ratzlaff, submitted to honor the 40th anniversary of the publication of *Celebration of Discipline*.

86 Andy Sloan, submitted to honor the 40th anniversary of the publication of *Celebration of Discipline*.

87 Janine Roberts, submitted to honor the 40th anniversary of the publication of *Celebration of Discipline*.

88 Dr. Grace Ju Miller, submitted to honor the 40th anniversary of the publication of *Celebration of Discipline*.

89 Leighton Ford, Leighton Ford Ministries. Submitted to honor the 40th anniversary of the publication of *Celebration of Discipline*.

90 Tony Campolo, author of *Who Switched the Price Tags* and *Seven Deadly Sins*. Submitted to honor the 40th anniversary of the publication of *Celebration of Discipline*.

91 Lisa Sharon Harper, speaker, writer, activist for social change, and founder of Freedom Road (Zoom interview dated 7/31/2020).

92 Foster, *Celebration of Discipline*, p. 1.

93 Richard J. Foster, *Streams of Living Water* (HarperSanFrancisco, 1998), p. 137.

94 Foster, *Celebration of Discipline*, p. 134.

95 Foster, *Celebration of Discipline*, p. 129.

96 Tina Dyer, email submitted on December 18, 2021.

97 Evan Howard, "Evangelical Spirituality," in *Four Views of Christian Spirituality*, ed. Bruce Demarest (Grand Rapids: Zondervan, 2012).

98 Richard Foster, *Celebration of Discipline: The Path to Spiritual Growth*, Special Ten Year Anniversary Edition, p. 8.

99 Dave Hunt & T.A. McMahon, *The Seduction of Christianity* (Harvest House, 1985), pp.173–174.

100 The Berean Call website.

101 David Nelson, "Syncretism in the Church: Satanism in the land? Part II", *The Shield: A Ministry to Non-Christian Religions and Aberrant Christian Groups*, Vol.4, Number 1, March 1990.

102 Ray Yungen, *A Time of Departing* (Lighthouse Trails Research Project website), ch. 4.

103 Albert James Dager, "Renovaré Spiritual Formation Groups on the Rise," *Media Spotlight Special Report*, January 31, 1992, p. 3.

104 Ibid, p. 4.

105 Elliot Miller, Editor-in-Chief, "Letter to the Editor of The Shield," Editor-in-Chief, *Christian Research Journal*, Christian Research Institute, July 15, 1990.

106 Interview with Richard Foster," Bob Latta, "Religion Today" staff writer *The Wichita Eagle*, December 10, 1979.

107 "Syncretism Part III: Is A *Celebration of Discipline* Really That Bad?" Dr. Craig Blomberg, *The Shield*, Spring 1991.

108 *Embracing Contemplation: Reclaiming a Christian Spiritual Practice*, ed. John H. Coe and Kyle C. Strobel (IVP Academic, 2019), p. 95.

109 Dallas Willard, *Defense of Visualization Against Certain Theological Objections*. 1988 Dallas Willard Family Trust. (see Appendix E).

110 Todd Dean Hunter is an American author, church planter, and bishop in the Anglican Church in North America. (Zoom interview September 23, 2020).

111 Richard F. Lovelace, *Dynamics of Spiritual Life: An Evangelical Theology of Renewal* (Downers Grove, IL: InterVarsity Press, 1979), p. 232, quoted in *Embracing Contemplation*, p. 2.

112 Stephen D. Boyer and Christopher A. Hall, *The Mystery of God: Theology for Knowing the Unknowable* (Baker Academic, 2012), Galatians 5:22, p. 198.

113 David Pocta, "A Critical Reflection in Spirituality: Richard Foster—Leading You into the Fold, or Leading You Astray?" (Oblate School of Theology).

114 George M. Marsden, *C.S. Lewis' Mere Christianity: A Biography* (Princeton University Press, 2016), p. 1.

115 Bob Latta, "Religion Today" staff writer *The Wichita Eagle*, December 10, 1979.

116 Richard Foster, "Casting a Vision: The Past and Future of Spiritual Formation," George Fox Renovaré Pastor's Conference, June 2018, pp. 1, 2.

117 Richard J. Foster, *Streams of Living Water: Celebrating the Great Traditions of Christian Faith* (HarperSanFrancisco, 1998). pp. 273–274.

118 Charles Moore, *Called to Community*, pp. xv–xvii.

119 *Called to Community*, p. 15.

120 *Called to Community*, pp. 88–90.

121 James Bryan Smith, *The Good and Beautiful Community*, (Intervarsity Press, 2010), p. 85.

122 Foster, *Celebration*, p. 164.

123 Foster, *Celebration*, pp. 131, 132.

124 Averbeck, R.E. (2008) Spirit, community, and mission: A biblical theology for spiritual formation. *Journal of Spiritual Formation and Soul Care*, 1 (1), 27–53.

125 Bradley P. Holt, *Thirsty for God: A Brief History of Christian Spirituality*, Third Edition (Fortress Press, 2017), p. 21.

126 1 Timothy 4:7–8; Romans 12:2; Ephesians 4:22–24; 2 Corinthians 3:18, 4:16; Colossians 3:10–11.

127 "Spiritual Formation," Wikipedia, April 30, 2020.

128 David Pocta, "A Critical Reflection in Spirituality: Richard Foster—Leading You into the Fold or Leading You Astray?" (Oblate School of Theology).

129 Gerald L. Sittser, *Water from a Deep Well: Christian Spirituality from Early Martyrs to Modern Missionaries* (IVP Books, 2007), p. 18.

130 Howard Baker, ThM, is Assistant Professor of Christian Formation; Director of Christian Formation at Denver Seminary. He is author of *The One True Thing* and *Soul Keeping*.

131 Interview with Richard Foster: *"Celebration of Discipline,"* by Grace Christus, *Eternity* magazine Fall 1981. p. 70.

132 Valerie Hess written comments, 8/1/2020; follow-up Zoom interview on 11/12/2020.

133 Richard Hovey, Renovaré Canada (July 21, 2020 email).

134 Richard J. Foster's original proposal written in 1991.

135 *A Call to Spiritual Formation*, 2009. Appendix D.

136 Matthew 11:19 NIV.

137 Jefferey Rediger, M.D., *Cured: The Life-Changing Science of Spontaneous Healing* (Flatiron Books, 2020), p. 364.

138 Dr. Gayle D. Beebe is a college professor, President of Westmont College in Santa Barbara, CA, and writer.

139 Richard J. Foster and Gayle D. Beebe, *Longing for God: Seven Paths of Christian Devotion* (IVP Formatio, 2009).

140 Nancy Thomas, "Remembering Richard Foster and *Celebration of Discipline,"* email submission March 26, 2020.

141 Siang Yang Tan is a pastor, professor at Fuller Seminary in the School of Psychology, bestselling author, and esteemed member of Renovaré's Ministry Team.

142 Gary R. Collins, Professor of Psychology, Trinity Evangelical Divinity School. Submitted to honor the 10th anniversary of the publication of *Celebration of Discipline*.

143 Valerie Hess, author. Submission of written comments, 8/1/2020; follow-up Zoom interview on 11/12/2020.

144 Jon Kohan, political consultant; email submission, June 11, 2020.

145 Audrey and Robert Chestnut. Submitted to honor the 40th anniversary of the publication of *Celebration of Discipline*.

146 Marti Ensign, Renovaré Ministry Team member, email submission April 8, 2020.

147 Arends is currently serving as Renovaré's Director of Education. Quotes are taken from Carolyn Arends article, "ReArrangements: Transforming Habits: Why Spiritual Disciplines Are Worth Celebrating" (*Today's Christian Woman*, April 29, 2016).

148 Reverend Doctor Derek Oppenshaw, Supernumerary Minister, Methodist Church of Southern Africa, 2021. The full article created and submitted for this book biography may be found in Appendix D.

149 Andrew Arndt, Pastor of New Life Church in Colorado Springs, Colorado. Submitted in two emails, May 13, 2020, and January 9, 2023.

150 Submitted by Korean Pastor Joshua Choonmin Kang (Senior Pastor of L.A. New Life Vision Church), email, July 20, 2020.

151 J.P. Moreland, *Finding Quiet* (Zondervan, 2019), pp. 66–67.

152 Katherine Thompson, *Christ-Centred Mindfulness: Connection to Self and God* (Acorn Press, 2018), p. 45.

153 Romans 12:2 NIV.

154 Childre, Doc, and Deborah Rozman. *Transforming Stress: the HeartMath Solution for Relieving Worry, Fatigue, and Tension.* Oakland, CA: New Harbinger, 2005, p. 31.

155 J.P. Moreland, *Finding Quiet* (Zondervan, 2019), p. 140.

156 Thompson, *Anatomy of the Soul*, p. 94, 95.

157 Jeffrey Rediger, *Cured: The Life-Changing Science of Spontaneous Healing* (Flat Iron Books, NY, 2020), p. 151.

158 Herbert Alfononso, S.J. *Discovering Your Personal Vocation* (Paulist Press, 2001), p. 52.

159 Michael L. Birkel, *Silence and Witness: The Quaker Tradition* (Orbis Books, NY 2004), p. 45.

160 Caroline E. Stephen, *Light Arising: Thoughts on the Central Radiance* (Cambridge: W. Heffer & Sons, 1980), pp. 68–69.

161 Thompson, *Anatomy of the Soul*, p. 99.

162 Quoted by George Marsden in *C.S. Lewis's Mere Christianity: a Biography* (Princeton University Press, 2016), p. 171.

163 Richard Foster, *Celebration of Discipline* fortieth anniversary edition, pp. xiii–xvii.

164 I am indebted to George Marsden for this apt depiction.

165 Dallas Willard, *The Divine Conspiracy: Rediscovering Our Hidden Life with God* (HarperSanFrancisco, 1997) pp. 41, 45.

166 C.S. Lewis, "The Funeral of a Great Myth," in *Christian Reflections*, pp. 82–93.

167 Brandon Vogt, bestselling author and Senior Publishing Director for Bishop Robert Barron's *Word on Fire Catholic Ministries*.

168 William Penn, *No Cross, No Crown* (1682).

169 See Chapter 8.

170 Appendix E is an excerpt written by Richard Foster from the 1983 *Celebration of Discipline* Study Guide outlining, "The Danger of Spiritual Disciplines: Seven Pitfalls to Avoid."

171 Foster, *Celebration of Discipline*, foreword to 40th anniversary edition, pp. xiii–xiv.

172 Foster, *Celebration*, p. 163.

173 Richard J. Foster, *Celebration of Discipline: the Path to Spiritual Growth* (Harper & Row, 1978), p. 1.

174 174 Richard J. Foster, Celebration of Discipline: The Path to Spiritual Growth, Special 40th Anniversary Edition,

(HarperOne, 2018), "The Great Conversation: An Annotated Bibliography," p. 203ff

175   Quoted in the fortieth edition of Celebration of Discipline, p.213

176   Devotional Classics: Selected Readings for Individuals and Groups, (HarperOne Revised and Expanded Edition, 2005), edited by Richard J. Foster and James Bryan Smith.

177   Spiritual Classics: Selected Readings on the Twelve Spiritual Disciplines (HarperOne, 2000), edited by Richard J. Foster and Emilie Griffin.

178   David Le Shana, president of George Fox College, *Newberg Graphic*, Thursday, June 22, 1978.

179   Florence Lawson, *Palladium-Item* Religion Writer, December 16, 1979.

180   Jack L. Wilcuts, *The Friend*, 8/18/1979.

181   Hart Armstrong, *For Defenders Friends*, Fall 1979.

182   Timothy K. Jones, *Quarterly Review*, (Church of the Brethren), Summer 1987.

183   Paul L. Morell, UM Minister, *Good News Magazine*, March/April 1986.

184   William C. Frey, bishop, Episcopal Diocese of Colorado. Submitted to honor the 10th anniversary of the publication of *Celebration of Discipline*.

185   Peter Prime, associate secretary of the General Conference Ministerial Association, *Adventist Review*, January 19, 2006.

186   Quoted by Edward England, *The Unfading Vision*, p. 120.

187   Charles J. Healey, S.J., *Review for Religious*, Vol. 38, 1979/4.

188   *San Francisco Catholic*, March 1987.

189   Sister Ann Rita Murphy, G.N.S.H., *Sisters Today, The Grey Nuns Motherhouse*, Yardley, Pennsylvania, August/September 1978.

190   The Reverend Alan Cadwallader, Anglican Vicar of St. Georges, Flemington, Victoria. *Christian Book Newsletter*, March 1988.

191 John Pearce, *Church of England Newspaper*, January 9, 1981.

192 Geoffrey M. Young, *Herald*, July 1, 1989.

193 *The Friend* [London], December 1979.

194 Brian Hoare, Cliff College UK, *The Evangelical Quarterly*.

195 Derek Fields, *Restoration*, May/June 1981.

196 John Cockerton, Wheldrake Rectory, York; *Churchman*, Vol. 95, No. 3.

197 Keith Walker, *British Church Times, (Hodder & Stoughton edition)*, December 19, 1980.

198 *Australian Evangel*, Hodder Australia, July 1989.

199 Gordon Preece, *Australian Church Record*, Feb. 21, 1983.

200 Christianity Today article, "The Ministry of the Towel: Practicing Love through Service," January 7, 1983.

201 "Many Choices on the Menu of Religious Fasts," Mark Oppenheimer, *New York Times*, January 22, 2011.

202 *Creation and Hope* edited by Nicola Hoggard Creegan and Andrew Shepherd. (Pickwick publications, Wipf and Stock, Oregon, 2018), cited *Celebration of Discipline* on page 159.

203 "Religion on Campus," *Liberal Education Periodical*, January 4, 2002, cited *Celebration of Discipline* on p. 33.

204 *Christianity Today* cover article: "Chastity is a spiritual discipline for the whole church," May 2005 (Lauren F. Winner is author of *Real Sex: The Naked Truth about Chastity* [Brazos, 2005]. *Christianity Today*, May 2005)

205 Katherine Thompson, *Christ Centred Mindfulness: Connection to Self and God* (Acorn Press, 2018), p. 83, 100–101.

206 Ken Shigematsu, *God in My Everything* (Zondervan, 2013), pp. 55, 131.

207 Howard Baker, *Soul Keeping: Ancient Paths of Spiritual Direction* (Navpress, 1998), cited on pp. 92, 131; *The One True Thing* (Navpress, 2007), cited on p. 124.

208 Ruth Haley Barton, *Invitation to Solitude and Silence* (IVP, 2004) and *Sacred Rhythms* (IVP, 2006).

209 David Benner, *Sacred Companions* (IVP, 2002), cited on pp. 209, 217.

210 Adele Ahlberg Calhoun, *Spiritual Disciplines Handbook* (IVP, 2005).

211 Peter Greig, *The Vision and the Vow* (Relevant Book, 2004), cited on p. xxi.

212 Valerie E. Hess, *Spiritual Disciplines Devotional* (IVP, 2007).

213 Jan Johnson, *Spiritual Disciplines Companion* (IVP, 2009), cited on pp. 47, 60, 128, 164, 169.

214 M. Robert Mulholland Jr., *Invitation to a Journey* (IVP Books, 1993); cited on p. 102.

215 John Ortberg, *The Life You've Always Wanted: Spiritual Disciplines for Ordinary People* (Zondervan,1997, 2002), cited on pp.44,81,113; and *Soul Keeping* (Zondervan, 2014), cited on p. 56.

216 James Bryan Smith, *Apprentice* series published by IVP: *The Good and Beautiful God* (2009) cites *Celebration of Discipline* on pp. 10, 61, 183; *The Good and Beautiful Life* (2009) cites *Celebration of Discipline* on p.166; *The Good and Beautiful Community* (2010), cites *Celebration of Discipline* on pp. 159, 186.

217 Dallas Willard, *The Divine Conspiracy: Understanding How God Changes Lives* (Harper & Row, 1998), cited on p. 17.

218 Note: The four-part film series has been combined and is available for viewing on YouTube.

219 Roy M. Carlisle, "A Catholic Bestseller Backstory, *Celebration of Discipline*," Roth Advertising, Inc. 2/22/2010.

220 Telephone interview with Lyle Smith-Graybeal.

221 Richard J. Foster author.

222 Richard J. Foster, *Celebration of Discipline* (HarperSanFrancisco, 1988), pp. 25–26.

223 David A. Seamands, *Healing of the Memories*, (Wheaton, IL, Victor Books, 1985), pp. 61–62.

224 (c) 1988 Dallas Willard Family Trust. Used by permission.

225 Cf. Ps 5:3; 119:147; Mark 1:35.

226 Cf. (Foster, 2005:2).

227 Consuming only certain vegetables, fruits, whole grains, legumes, nuts, and seeds.

228 Commences after the evening meal and breaking at the "traditional afternoon tea."

229 Because Richard Foster is a Quaker.

230 Cf. *Spiritual Bedfellows? The Quaker-Methodist Connection* (aquakerstew.blogspot.com).

Author photo: Bettinger Photography
in Denver, Colorado

Miriam (Mimi) Dixon began her ministry in 1979 serving as an associate pastor at Northminster Presbyterian Church in Seattle, Washington. From April of 1985 to May of 2019, she served as senior pastor of First Presbyterian Church of Golden, Colorado. She earned both her MDiv and DMin degrees from Fuller Theological Seminary. Mimi is on the Renovaré Board of Directors and teaches for the Renovaré Institute. She is faculty for Next Frontiers, a ministry to pastors in transition, and actively promotes Christian Spiritual Formation, crediting Richard Foster and Dallas Willard for their influence in her life and ministry.